RANDOM HARVEST

by

JAMES HILTON

Dramatized by

MOIE CHARLES and BARBARA TOY

D0862505

LONDON
SAMUEL FRENCH LIMITED

FOR AMATEUR PRODUCTION ENQUIRIES

UNITED KINGDOM AND WORLD EXCLUDING NORTH AMERICA

plays@SamuelFrench-London.co.uk

020 7255 4302/01

Each title is subject to availability from Samuel French,

depending upon country of performance.

RANDOM HARVEST

Produced at Theatre Royal, Brighton, on October 25th, 1948, with the following cast of characters :—

CHETWYND RAINIER	*Michael Logan*
LYDIA RAINIER (*Chetwynd's wife*)	*Frances Clare*
JILL NORTH (*Chetwynd's sister*)	*Marjorie Stewart*
GEORGE RAINIER (*Chetwynd's younger brother*)	*Michael Bilton*
KITTY NORTH (*Jill's step-daughter*)	*Margaret Anderson*
SHELDON (*The butler*)	*Norman Macowan*
ELSIE (*The tweeny-maid*)	*Mary Merrett*
TRUSLOVE (*A solicitor*)	*John Miller*
CHARLES RAINIER (*Chetwynd's youngest brother*)	*Dermot Walsh*
HELEN HASLETT	*Hazel Court*
HARRISON (*An undergraduate*)	*Clive Baxter*
THE DUCHESS OF CHELSEA	*Kathleen Gerrard*

The Play produced by Peter Creswell.

SYNOPSIS OF SCENES

PROLOGUE. Euston Station. December, 1920. Night.

ACT I

SCENE 1.—The study of Stourton, the Rainiers' house in the country. The next day. Late afternoon.

SCENE 2.—The same. June, 1922. Noon.

ACT II

SCENE 1.—The same. April, 1925. Afternoon.

SCENE 2.—The same. September, 1932. Afternoon.

ACT III

SCENE 1.—The same. August, 1938. Evening.

SCENE 2.—The same. Later the same night.

To face page 1—*Random Harvest*

RANDOM HARVEST

PROLOGUE

SCENE.—*A departure platform at Euston Station, London. A night early in December, 1920.*

Only one compartment door is visible C. *through the murky gloom and fog enveloping the rest of the carriage and the departure platform.*

When the CURTAIN *rises, the stage is in darkness. Lights fade in on the carriage door, and a man and a woman become visible. The woman, who will later call herself* HELEN HASLETT, *is* PAULA, *and it is important that throughout the Prologue her face should not be seen by the audience ; the man,* CHARLES RAINIER, *is known to* PAULA *in the Prologue as* SMITHY. *He climbs into the compartment.* HELEN *hustles him in and shuts the door. She stands gazing up at him. She is aged twenty. She wears a big coat and a little fur cap, and carries a handbag and a bunch of violets.* CHARLES *leans out of the window ; the pallid foggy light only just picks out his face. He is in his early twenties, but looks older. There is a free and happy air about him. Once or twice during the scene, he stammers very slightly.*

HELEN. You're sure you'll be all right in there ?

CHARLES. I'll be fine. I've got a corner seat.

HELEN. I still wish you weren't travelling overnight.

CHARLES. But it gave us the whole evening together first. Or rather, (*he laughs*) you gave me the most wonderful evening. Can you beat it ? We go out for the evening and I forget my wallet.

HELEN. It's been heaven, hasn't it, darling ? Little Tich and all. My face is still in the most terrible mess from laughing so much.

(CHARLES *leans down and kisses her.*)

CHARLES. I think your face is lovely.

HELEN. What time do you get into Liverpool ?

CHARLES. Last time I asked you, you said four thirty-one, which probably means some time after five a.m.

HELEN. You'll be sure to get yourself a good breakfast—promise ?

CHARLES. I promise. I've got to bolster myself up somehow to meet the editor chap.

HELEN. Oh, isn't it wonderful, Smithy ? It's like a fairy tale come true. You write and write and nothing happens . . .

CHARLES. Except every word keeps getting slung back at me.

HELEN. And all of a sudden an editor in Liverpool likes a whole lot of your articles.

1

CHARLES. He's got to do more than like 'em. He's got to buy them and a whole lot more.

HELEN. We'll have some money. We could even move from our attic.

CHARLES. I'd much rather stay on there.

HELEN. I'd like to stay, too. I love our attic in that ugly old house. Oh, darling !

CHARLES (*seriously*). You are glad you married me, Paula ?

HELEN. Glad ? (*She laughs.*) After the time I had chasing you, you hadn't a chance of not marrying me. Oh, Smithy !

CHARLES. What ?

HELEN. I wish I was going with you. Somehow I feel—at this moment I *should* go with you.

CHARLES. But darling, it's only for a couple of days. The fare costs such a lot.

HELEN. I know. I'm silly. You won't start getting fussed or bothered or worried because you're on your own ?

CHARLES. Of course not. It's just that it's the first time.

HELEN. Do you still try and remember who you really are ?

CHARLES. Sometimes—yes.

HELEN. But you don't worry about it ?

CHARLES. No, not really. But it's no small thing to forget—twenty odd years. I wonder who I am ; where I come from. Details *you* should know. Why, I may be a thug, a . . .

HELEN (*with simple pride*). No, Smithy. You're a gentleman. I know that.

CHARLES (*a little panic stricken*). And if my memory should come back ? What then ?

HELEN. Why, darling, what then ?

CHARLES. You'll be there, you wouldn't leave me ? You . . .

HELEN. I'll be there, Smithy.

CHARLES. Promise ?

HELEN. I promise.

CHARLES. Cross your heart ?

HELEN. Cross my heart. (*She pauses.*) What does it feel like—to think of the time before—before you can remember ?

CHARLES. Like trying to remember before I was born. Everything began with you, and everything goes on with you—there's nothing else, Paula.

HELEN. Oh, what a lovely thing to tell me. I know, (*she has a terrific thought*) when you come back, let's take a day off and go down to Beachings Over. We'll climb Mickle. And have lunch on the top of our own special mountain.

CHARLES (*excitedly*). And look down on all four counties. That ought to put the Liverpool editor in his right perspective.

HELEN. Five, Smithy. You can see five counties.

CHARLES. Five counties, then. I love you.

HELEN. It's like a miracle.

CHARLES. Take care of yourself.

HELEN. I will, duckie.

CHARLES. That's the first time you've said " duckie " for weeks.

HELEN. I know. I'm dropping it. Now I'm not an old pro any more, I don't have to talk like one.

CHARLES. I worry sometimes that you miss the stage.

HELEN. Never. They were playing our old show *Salute The Flag* at Penge last week. I passed the bills without a snivel. You see, darling, all I want is you. Can't believe there was a time when I didn't know you.

CHARLES. And yet it's a very short time that we have known each other.

HELEN. We've been married a whole year and two months.

CHARLES. Yes ! October seventh. That was a day !

HELEN. Seven always was my lucky number. (*She nods.*) I'm so happy.

(*A whistle is blown off.*)

(*She opens her handbag and takes out a handkerchief.*) Sure you've got enough money ?

CHARLES. Quite sure. I've taken your last penny, anyway. But you'll find some in my wallet, darling—it's probably on the dressing-table.

HELEN. Are you sure you're warm enough ? I *do* wish you'd wear an overcoat.

CHARLES (*grinning*). Fuss ! Fuss !

HELEN. The violets still smell. (*She holds them up to him.*) Smell.

CHARLES (*leaning down and sniffing at the violets*). H'mm. They do. I love seeing them on you. I'll always give them to you.

(*A whistle is blown off.*)

HELEN (*impulsively*). I'm mad to let you go alone. I should come with you.

CHARLES. I'm all right. See you the day after tomorrow.

(*The noise of the train beginning to move is heard.*)

Good-bye, my love. (*He kisses her.*)

HELEN. Good-bye, Smithy. Come back soon.

The LIGHTS *dim to* BLACK-OUT. *The noise of a departing train is heard as—*

the CURTAIN *falls.*

ACT I

SCENE 1

SCENE.—*The study of Stourton, the Rainiers' house in the country. The next day. Late afternoon.*

The study is a medium-sized, gracious room with tall windows in a bay up L. *and tall french windows down* L. *As Stourton was built by a pupil of Sir Christopher Wren, the large fireplace,* C. *of the wall* R., *is in keeping with the period. Double doors back* C. *open on to a vista of pillared hall. The view from the windows is of beautiful gardens with wide rolling parklands and a line of hills in the distance.* R. *and* L. *of the doors up* C. *are well-filled, built-in bookcases. Below the fireplace, there is a drinks table with an armchair above it. Above the fireplace, a small pedestal table with a large tallboy above it. A second armchair stands down* L. *Up* L.C., *near the window bay, a large carved desk is set at an angle. It has a high-backed armchair behind it and a duet stool in front of it. Three Queen Anne chairs stand, one* R. *of the door up* C., *one* L. *of the door, and one above the french windows. A settee stands* R.C. *at right-angles to the fireplace. There is a low coffee table below the settee and a pouffe down* R.C. *The room is comfortably carpeted and curtained. Electric candle wall brackets* R. *and* L. *of the door up* C., *and above the french windows provide lighting. The switch is* L. *of the door. A bell is in the wall above the fireplace. One or two good pictures hang on the walls. There is a brass kerb and fire-irons at the fireplace.*

(See the Ground Plan at the end of the Play.)

When the CURTAIN *rises, there is a bright log fire burning in the iron fire basket. It is late afternoon, and is grey and cheerless outside. The lights have not been lit.* CHETWYND RAINIER *is seated at the* R. *end of the settee. He is a big man, over-hearty and in his forties.* LYDIA, *his wife, is seated* L. *of him. She is an ambitious, but frustrated woman.* GEORGE RAINIER *is a small, quiet man, and is seated down* L. *He has a cup and saucer in his hand.* JILL NORTH *is standing gazing out of the french windows. She is aged about twenty-five and is smartly dressed.* KITTY, *her step-daughter, is seated on the pouffe with her back to the audience. She is an intelligent girl of fifteen.* CHETWYND *hands his empty cup to* LYDIA.

JILL (*shivering*). Good old England ! Grey and cheerless as usual.

LYDIA (*placing* CHETWYND'S *cup and saucer on the tray*). Dear Jill, we can't all live on the Riviera the whole year round. Most of us have to put up with England, whether we like it or not. (*She peers into the teapot.*)

4

To face page 4—Random Harvest

CHETWYND. Didn't like having to cable you, Jill. (*To* LYDIA.) Did we, old girl ? (*To* JILL.) But as the old man seemed dangerously ill this time, Lydia and I felt you ought to be told. Besides, he wanted the family round him, and all that.

JILL (*crossing to the armchair down* R.). Of course, Chet. I understand. (*She sits and places her handbag on the floor beside her.*)

LYDIA. Ring the bell, Kitty. (*She pours out a cup of tea for* CHETWYND *and passes it to him.*)

(KITTY *does not move or answer.*)

JILL. Kitty !

KITTY (*rising reluctantly*). Aunt Lydia can reach the bell.

JILL. Kitty, will you *please* do as you're told.

KITTY (*moving above the fireplace*). All right, Mother. (*She rings the bell.*)

JILL. Kitty, please ! (*To* CHETWYND.) Father's had these relapses before, but I suppose this one's more serious than usual.

KITTY (*wandering to the french windows*). Anyway, it was worth it. I got the whole weekend off from school to come and see you. Missed the maths exam, too.

GEORGE. Father's as strong as a horse, really.

CHETWYND. Wish I had his constitution. His illness has meant a lot of responsibility for me one way and another. But everything's going damn well. Never realized till father got ill, how easy it is to cope with big business.

KITTY (*gazing through the french windows*). The light from the window sort of beckons across the lawn.

JILL. How is business, Chet ?

CHETWYND. Booming, old girl, booming. And the war's only been over two years. God knows how much more it'll boom.

LYDIA. My dear, Jill only wants to know whether she will get her dividends or not.

CHETWYND (*to* JILL). Don't worry, little sister, all the family will collect a handsome pile this year.

JILL. Then back I go to the South of France and sunshine.

LYDIA. And attractive dancing partners.

JILL (*good-naturedly*). Naturally. Men are quite their most attractive when they're sunburnt. I wish you could see Maurice diving . . .

LYDIA. Jill, really !

JILL. He's like a young Apollo. Well, the Kaiser stole four years from me, and now I'm making up for them.

(KITTY *turns and wanders* C.)

LYDIA. What about Kitty ?

(KITTY *wanders to the french windows.*)

JILL. She's got two more years at school.

A*

LYDIA. Kitty! I wish you wouldn't wander around. We haven't finished tea, even if you have.

KITTY. Sorry!

(SHELDON, *the butler, enters up* C. *He is a Scotsman and is the complete dignified gentleman. He carries a silver kettle of hot water.*)

SHELDON (*closing the door behind him*). You rang, Mrs Chetwynd ?

LYDIA (*without looking at* SHELDON). Some more hot water, please, Sheldon.

SHELDON (*moving to the fireplace*). I thought as much. (*He places the kettle on its stand in the hearth.*)

KITTY. Stourton is dreadfully large, isn't it ?

CHETWYND. Your Aunt Lydia got lost for three hours the first time I brought her here. (*He drinks his tea.*)

(SHELDON *moves* C.)

GEORGE (*rising ; trying to excuse* LYDIA). Don't blame you. (*He moves to the desk.*) Must have been a bit of a maze after the vicarage. (*He puts his empty cup and saucer on the desk and sits on the duet stool.*)

CHETWYND (*before* LYDIA *can wither* GEORGE). Can't say I ever thought about it. Comes of being born here, what ?

KITTY. I wish *I* had been born here. I wish I was really part of the family and of Stourton.

(*This softens* SHELDON *to* KITTY *considerably. He gives her an approving look.*)

The grounds seem to go on for ever.

SHELDON (*easing up* C.). As far as you can see, Miss Kitty, even on a clear day.

KITTY (*moving to* L. *of* SHELDON). Is Stourton terribly old, Sheldon ?

LYDIA. Really, Kitty, why ask Sheldon ?

KITTY (*linking her right arm into* SHELDON's *left arm*). He always knows everything.

JILL. I remember when we were children, whatever problem cropped up, Charles always used to say—" Let's leave it to Sheldon."

KITTY (*moving down* L.C. ; *excitedly*). You mean Uncle Charles —you mean the one who was killed in the war ?

JILL (*motioning* KITTY *to be quiet*). Yes, yes, Kitty, but not so loud.

CHETWYND. Poor old Charles.

GEORGE. Good chap.

JILL (*directing her remark at* SHELDON). Even though he was always the favourite.

KITTY (*almost to sympathize with* SHELDON). How old is Stourton, Sheldon ?

SHELDON (*easing* R. *of the door up* C.). About two hundred years, miss. Said to have been built by a pupil of Sir Christopher Wren.

(*The door up* C. *opens, and* ELSIE, *a very young diminutive tweeny-maid, enters backwards, bumping the door open with her behind. She wears an old overall, black, torn stockings, and her face is very dirty. With both hands she lugs a scuttle of coal.*)

(*He looks at* ELSIE, *horrified.*) Outside.

(KITTY *eases* R. *of the desk.*)

ELSIE.   But, Mr Sheldon . . .

SHELDON.   Outside. You must never be seen by company. You're not ready.

(*He shoos* ELSIE *through the door up* C. *and they both exit,* SHELDON *closing the door behind them.*)

KITTY (*easing down* L.C.).   Poor old Sheldon.

LYDIA.   He's the last person to need pity.

KITTY.   But he's sort of like a tree that's half been struck by lightning.

CHETWYND (*placing his cup on the tray*).   Come to think of it, he's never been the same since we heard Charles was missing, has he, Jill ? (*He rises, moves to the fireplace and stands with his back to it.*)

JILL.   Suppose he hasn't.

KITTY.   But he can't still think about him. Why, Uncle Charles was killed nearly three years ago.

CHETWYND.   Good Lord, is it as long as all that ? Must be.

KITTY.   The most exciting thing was when he was mentioned in despatches prematurely.

JILL (*smiling*).   Posthumously, darling.

GEORGE (*wagging a finger at* KITTY).   Post—after. Latin. Latin.

(KITTY *doesn't even hear* GEORGE. *She moves* C. *and takes the stage.*)

KITTY (*quoting*).   " Despite intensive shelling, Captain Rainier, showing complete disregard for his own safety, was last seen leading his men against a heavily manned sector of the enemy line."

LYDIA.   Seems you know all there is to know about it.

KITTY.   I looked it up in an old *Gazette*. Uncle Charles sounds awfully thrilling.

CHETWYND.   He wasn't, I can tell you. He was damn quiet.

GEORGE.   Bit of a hero, all the same.

JILL (*to* KITTY).   He wasn't your real uncle, anyway, and while we're on the subject, I wish you wouldn't call me " mother ". Just because I married your father it doesn't make me your mother— you know I hate it. Anyway, I couldn't possibly have had a daughter of your age.

KITTY (*moving above the settee ; impulsively*).   Sorry—I keep forgetting.

(TRUSLOVE, *the family solicitor, enters up* C. *He is elderly, but has much sound wisdom about him. He is given to taking snuff.*)

TRUSLOVE (*moving* C.). I hope I don't intrude.

CHETWYND (*moving above the settee to* R. *of* TRUSLOVE). Of course not. Come on in, Truslove. How do you think the patient seems today ?

TRUSLOVE (*taking his snuff box from his pocket*). Not too good, I fear. Mr Rainier hardly recognized me. (*He takes a pinch of snuff.*)

GEORGE. Poor old boy.

TRUSLOVE. Sad, very sad. Dr Sanderstead would only allow me to stay for two or three minutes. The doctor is still with him.

CHETWYND. I wouldn't try and worry the old man about details at a time like this.

TRUSLOVE. But as his legal adviser, I do feel, Mr Chetwynd, that we should consult him about the transfer of those shares. If I may say so, I think you are being a little over-optimistic about them.

CHETWYND (*moving above* TRUSLOVE *to* R. *of* GEORGE). Don't you believe it—it's just a little manipulation that'll make us a cool ten thousand without even bothering the old boy, eh, George ? (*To* GEORGE.) Telling me only yesterday, weren't you, how golf ran away with a packet ? Gleneagles and all that ?

TRUSLOVE. Nevertheless, I'd rather hold up the transaction until I can consult Mr Rainier.

CHETWYND (*moving to the armchair down* L. ; *heatedly*). If you feel like that about it—then we'll drop the whole matter. (*He sits.*)

LYDIA. It's been going on like this for months, with Chet having to carry everything on his shoulders and nobody helping him. Mr Truslove prevents him from putting over any business deals, and the family worry him to death. You never leave him alone. Money, money, money.

(*There is an awkward pause. Nobody knows what to say to this outburst.*)

KITTY (*suddenly*). When Mr Rainier dies, will you all be very rich ?

TRUSLOVE. Ahem ! The Rainier fortune is a very considerable one, young lady. Very considerable indeed.

KITTY (*to* TRUSLOVE). How many Rainier factories are there altogether ? (*She eases to* R. *of the coffee table.*)

GEORGE. Six.

CHETWYND (*grumpily*). Scattered all over the country—damned inconvenient from a travelling point of view.

KITTY (*attempting to steal a piece of icing from the cake*). But they all have something to do with steel, haven't they ?

(LYDIA *smacks* KITTY'S *hand.*)

(*She withdraws her hand quickly.*) Because Rainier shares are listed under steel in the Stock Market prices.

JILL. Really, Kitty !

KITTY (*moving and standing with her back to the fireplace*).   I'm not just being nosey.   I do really want to know, because ten of us at school clubbed together and bought some of the shares.   We look at the prices every morning.

(GEORGE *nods his agreement.*)

TRUSLOVE (*smiling*).   Good gracious me.

GEORGE (*to* KITTY).   Do the same myself.

LYDIA (*to* JILL).   I should definitely write to the headmistress if I were you and complain.

JILL.   It really is naughty, Kitty.   I don't pay enormous school fees for you to spend your time dabbling on the Stock Exchange.

KITTY.   Mother—I don't call putting up twenty-five shillings, dabbling.

TRUSLOVE (*to* CHETWYND).   I have those cheques in the library, Mr Chetwynd, if you'd be so good as to spare me a few minutes.

CHETWYND (*rising and moving to the door up* C.).   Oh, well, better get them over and done with.   Coming, George ?

(*He exits up* C., *leaving the door open.*   TRUSLOVE *turns to follow him off.*   GEORGE *rises.*)

JILL (*to* TRUSLOVE).   Not found that siskin's nest yet, Mr Truslove ?

TRUSLOVE (*pausing and turning*).   No, but I'm still hoping !

(*He shakes his head, chuckles and exits up* C., *leaving the door open.*   GEORGE *starts to follow him, then changes his mind, closes the door, turns and moves to the french windows.*)

LYDIA.   Aren't you going, George ?

GEORGE.   No.   Need some fresh air.

(*He exits by the french windows, leaving them slightly ajar.*)

LYDIA.   Old Truslove is so conservative.   (*Very definitely.*)   We shall see *real* progress once Chet has complete control.

JILL (*rising and crossing to the french windows*).   Chet's all right. But I've got a lot of faith in Truslove.   (*She closes the french windows.*)   Suppose it's because I've known him since I was a child. He used to take me birds'-nesting.   He's been looking for a siskin's nest for forty years.

KITTY (*laughing*).   Fancy you and old Truslove—birds'-nesting. Who did the climbing ?

JILL.   Me.   (*Suddenly.*)   Damn !   I forgot to ring up Victor about my dress.   (*She crosses down* R. *and picks up her handbag.*) You really should get father to move the telephone out of the hall, Lydia, it's so hellishly draughty there.   (*She moves to the door up* C.)

LYDIA (*rising*).   I shall change a great many things here.

(JILL *stops abruptly at the door and turns.*)

(She moves up C., *to* R. *of* JILL.)   When you think of the entertaining, the dinners . . .

JILL.   Well, get Sheldon on your side and your entertaining will be as easy as pie.

(KITTY *eases to* R. *of the coffee table and eyes the cake.*)

LYDIA.   Sheldon will do as he's told.

JILL.   We'll see.

(KITTY *attempts to pick a piece of icing off the cake.*)

LYDIA.   I suppose I'd better have a word with Dr Sanderstead before he goes.

(She exits up C., *leaving the door open.*)

JILL.   Kitty, what are you doing ?

KITTY *(starting guiltily).*   Nothing !

JILL.   Well, don't.

(She exits up C., *closing the door behind her.* KITTY *starts to pick again at the icing.* CHARLES *enters quietly by the french windows, closing them softly behind him. He wears a brand new suit of clothes. He looks around curiously, then eases* L.C. *and watches* KITTY *at the icing. After a few moments,* KITTY *senses someone is there, straightens up suddenly, then makes a grab and picks up the poker.)*

CHARLES *(after a pause).*   Hello.

KITTY *(weakly).*   W-what do you want ?

CHARLES.   It's cold outside and the glow of light from the window was inviting.

KITTY.   But . . .

CHARLES *(looking around).*   Just the same. *(To* KITTY.)   Who are you ?

KITTY.   M mo ?

CHARLES.   Yes, what's your name ?

KITTY.   Kitty.

CHARLES *(easing* R.C. *and looking around).*   And who do you belong to ?

KITTY.   Jill.   I'm her step-daughter.   Look here, I really think you'd better go.   I mean, Aunt Lydia or Uncle Chet might phone for the police if they found you here.   Aunt Lydia thinks the world of this silver tea service.   I think it's awful.

CHARLES.   So do I.

(SHELDON *enters up* C.)

KITTY.   Oh, Sheldon.   Thank goodness . . .

CHARLES.   Hello, Sheldon.

SHELDON *(moving* L.C. ; *uncertain in the half-light).*   Sir—— ?

CHARLES.   It's Charles—you know.   Charles who was . . .   Oh, God, I can't go into all that, but remember Sherlock Holmes—*your* Dr Watson—that Charles.

SHELDON. *Mr* Charles ! (*With all the warmth of meaning.*) Mr Charles !

CHARLES. Yes. Wouldn't you like to sit down for a minute ?

SHELDON (*unsteadily*). No, thank you, sir.

CHARLES (*moving to* R. *of* SHELDON). Will you tell this young woman it's quite safe to put the poker down. She thinks I'm a thief or something.

(KITTY *returns the poker to the hearth.*)

SHELDON. I can't believe it.

CHARLES. Well—neither can I.

(KITTY *moves to the pouffe and kneels on it.*)

SHELDON. I—I can't quite collect myself yet, Mr Charles—but I —I'd like to be the first to—well to—congratulate you.

CHARLES. Thanks—though I don't know whether congratula-tion's quite the word.

KITTY (*rising and moving to* R. *of* CHARLES). Uncle Charles !

SHELDON. It's so extraordinary to have you back with us. It's like . . .

KITTY. A resurrection. You're supposed to be dead.

SHELDON (*simply*). I've missed you. But where've you been these past three years ?

CHARLES (*quietly*). I don't know.

SHELDON. You don't know ! What's happened to you ?

CHARLES (*breaking down* L.). All I can tell you is that I was in Liverpool this morning, and don't ask why Liverpool, because I don't know any more than you do. But I had a devil of a headache from being knocked down by a car.

SHELDON. You were knocked down !

CHARLES (*moving up* L.). Yes. The driver of the car put me on a park bench, and when I came round he was anxious, naturally, to be off. He could see I wasn't hurt. (*He sits on the duet stool.*) It was raining, and I was very muddy.

SHELDON. You were alone ?

CHARLES (*nodding*). I wandered round for a while, trying to collect myself—sort things out—as it were. I remembered my name was Rainier and who I was. I bought a paper and then I realized that three years had elapsed—three years of which I knew nothing. (*He pauses.*)

(KITTY *moves to the armchair down* R. *and sits.*)

Then I realized I was wet through and very muddy. I went to one of those off-the-peg tailors and got this suit. Thirty shillings—not bad, is it ?

(SHELDON *looks at the suit distantly.*)

SHELDON. Was there no trace of anything to show what you were doing in Liverpool ?

CHARLES. That's the strange thing—no wallet—nothing.

SHELDON. No letter or other means of identification ? No tailor's label on your old coat ?

CHARLES (*smiling*). Not a thing, Sherlock Holmes—just some loose money and this handkerchief. That's the evidence—so help me, God.

SHELDON. But where were you before Liverpool ?

CHARLES. Before that, I can't remember a thing since—since all sorts of things I don't want to remember. The war—lying between the lines with shells bursting—years ago. There's a sort of dark corridor between then and this morning.

(*There is a pause.*)

SHELDON. Would you like a drink, Mr Charles ? You look a wee bit pale.

CHARLES (*rising*). No, thanks. Do I really look pale ? (*He eases* L.C.)

SHELDON. Just a wee bit. Maybe it's the light.

CHARLES. I think I'm tired. I've come a long way since—since this morning. But what you and I have got to worry about is the job of re-introducing me—so to speak. Any ideas ?

SHELDON. If you'll give me a little time, Mr Charles—I'm still rather . . .

CHARLES. I know—bumfoozled is the word old Sarah used to use.

SHELDON (*almost breaking down*). Fancy you remembering that.

CHARLES. What's happened to her ?

SHELDON. She's still in the village. But she's feeble the now.

CHARLES. Poor old girl. (*Suddenly.*) God, what are we gossiping like this for ?

SHELDON. I don't know. There are some important things I'll need to tell you. I fear you'll find the house a bit put about.

CHARLES. I know. I had a talk with the new man at the lodge. He thought I was the doctor from London. I'm sorry about father. I realize I couldn't have turned up at a more awkward moment—in some ways. Much rather have come when it's quiet—nobody here.

SHELDON. You mean—the family ?

CHARLES. Well, yes. A bit of a problem—how to let them know.

SHELDON. Aye. Well, we'll need to face it.

KITTY. *They* have to face it, you mean, Sheldon ?

SHELDON. Without a doubt, they'll be delighted to see you once they get over the surprise.

CHARLES (*easing down* L.). The surprise of finding I'm still alive ?

KITTY. It's like a miracle !

(CHARLES *stops abruptly, turns and looks at* KITTY *as though the phrase is familiar.*)

SHELDON. Well, after such an interval, and with no news . . .

CHARLES. I know. Suppose you think of something to tell them.
I'll leave it all to you.

SHELDON (*smiling*). I was about to suggest that. Can I say,
speaking for myself—to have you back . . .

CHARLES. I know. Thanks. Don't worry about me, Sheldon—
I know you're thinking I'm not behaving according to formula, but I
can't help it—not for the moment.

SHELDON. I doubt if there is any formula for what you must be
feeling, Mr Charles. (*He moves to the door up* C.) I'll away and
tell them.

(*He exits up* C., *closing the door behind him.* CHARLES *looks wearily
around. He seems rather lost.*)

KITTY. Does your mind seem sort of clouded, Uncle Charles ?

CHARLES (*moving to the settee*). On the contrary—certain things
are very clear—like headlamps along a road on a dark night. (*He
sits on the settee at the* L. *end of it*). *Too* clear ! While the rest is in
darkness. It'll all come right, I daresay.

KITTY. But you don't remember a thing that's happened to you
for the last three years ?

CHARLES. Not a thing.

KITTY. But how tremendous ! Then anything might have
happened.

CHARLES. How about giving me some tea ?

KITTY (*rising and moving to the coffee table*). Of course. I'm
afraid it's a bit cold. (*She pours out a cup of tea.*)

(CHARLES *looks around the room.*)

Surely you remember something ? Have you tried to remember ?
(*She sits on the settee,* R. *of* CHARLES.)

CHARLES (*softly*). I've been trying all day, and all I get is a sense
of bewildering loss.

KITTY. Loss ? Someone you've lost ?

(*There is a pause.*)

CHARLES (*rising and moving* C.). As I stood on the lawn, I could
see the firelight in here, and I almost expected someone to be waiting
to welcome me home. (*He looks around.*)

KITTY. But this is your home.

CHARLES. I know, but I wasn't meaning that.

KITTY. You were expecting a special someone here, Uncle
Charles ?

(*There is a pause.* CHARLES *shakes his head wearily, moves to the
settee and resumes his seat on it.*)

CHARLES. It doesn't matter. Tell me about the family. By the way, what's the matter with father ?

KITTY. Something to do with his heart. But I expect it's old age—he's awfully old. (*She pauses and looks anxiously at* CHARLES.) Do you feel all right, Uncle Charles ? You look sort of funny.

CHARLES. The tea's just what I need. Have there been any changes here ?

KITTY. You mean, in the house ? The old billiards room's been pulled down and two new ones built.

CHARLES. Two new billiards rooms ! Good God !

KITTY. And two new bathrooms. And Beauty's had six puppies. Jill says I can have one providing Uncle Chet will give me one without my asking.

(TRUSLOVE *enters up* C. CHARLES *rises*.)

TRUSLOVE (*moving to* CHARLES). This is a great day, Mr Charles, a great day. (*He shakes hands with* CHARLES.) I can hardly believe my eyes. Very glad to see you again. Very glad indeed.

CHARLES (*embarrassed*). How are you, Truslove ? I hear you've been allowing them to go all modern here. Two billiards rooms and two new bathrooms. From which I gather the family income remains—er—not so bad.

TRUSLOVE (*easing* L.). Like the barometer, Mr Charles—still rising.

(CHETWYND *enters up* C.)

CHETWYND (*moving to* L. *of* CHARLES). Well, old chap ! (*He shakes hands with* CHARLES.) And how are you ?

CHARLES. Hello, Chet. How are you ?

(TRUSLOVE *sits on the duet stool*.)

CHETWYND (*easing* L.C.). Got married since you were—since you were home last.

(LYDIA *enters up* C.)

Ah ! There you are, my dear.

(LYDIA *moves to* R. *of* CHARLES.)

(*To* CHARLES.) Want you to meet my wife, Lydia. Lydia—this is Charles. (*He moves down* L.)

CHARLES (*disliking* LYDIA). How do you do ? (*He shakes hands with her.*)

(JILL *enters excitedly up* C. LYDIA *moves below the pouffe.*)

JILL. Charles, darling ! (*She moves to* CHARLES, *throws her arms around his neck and kisses him.*) You could have knocked me down with a sprig of heather when Sheldon told us. It's just too wonderful. I can't tell you how—how—how thrilled I am to see you. I've been married again—*and* widowed, darling. So sad. The most marvellous man—left me such a nice house in Cannes and—oh, yes Kitty, of course. This is my stepdaughter, Kitty.

KITTY. Uncle Charles knows all about me. I was the first one to see him alive—wasn't I, Uncle Charles ?

(CHARLES *smiles at* KITTY.)

CHETWYND. Too bad father's ill. We ought to have had a party or something to celebrate the return of the long-lost son.

(CHARLES *sits on the settee, at the* L. *end of it.*)

CHARLES. I'm sorry he's ill—but not for that reason, I assure you.

(GEORGE *enters by the french windows. He carries a golf club.*)

GEORGE (*putting the club on the desk*). Just putted the seventh in one.

CHARLES. Hello, George.

GEORGE (*easing down* L.C.). Eh ?

CHARLES. It's me—Charles.

KITTY. It's Uncle Charles, the one who got killed.

GEORGE. It's brother Charles !

CHETWYND. Yes, old boy ! Charles come back after all this time.

GEORGE. Oh, I say ! (*He staggers a little and puts his hand to his head.*)

CHETWYND (*moving quickly to* GEORGE). Take it easy, old chap. (*He leads* GEORGE *to the armchair down* L.) Sit down.

(GEORGE *s ts.*)

How about a drop of brandy ?

(JILL *moves quickly to the drinks table down* R., *and pours out a brandy.* LYDIA *crosses to* L. *and fusses around* GEORGE.)

KITTY (*rising and moving to* JILL). I think Uncle George thought he was seeing a ghost.

JILL (*giving the glass to* KITTY). Well, suppose you give him this.

(KITTY *crosses to* L. *and gives the glass to* GEORGE.)

GEORGE (*taking the glass*). Oh, thank you. (*He drinks.*) That's much better. Bit of a shock, what ? (*He gives the empty glass to* KITTY.)

LYDIA. It certainly is.

(*There is an awkward pause. Nobody seems to have anything to say.* KITTY *moves up* L. *and puts the glass on the desk.*)

CHARLES (*rising and moving* R.C.). I feel I owe you all sorts of explanations, but the fact is, this whole business of coming back, is as big a mystery to me as it must be to you. I suppose loss of memory's like that—but I do want to tell you I'm a perfectly normal person, so far as everyday things are concerned. I'm not ill, and you don't have to treat me with any special consideration.

(KITTY *moves to* L. *of* CHARLES.)

JILL (*moving to the settee*). We understand, Charles. (*She sits on the settee, at the* L. *end of it.*)

CHETWYND. Course, quite understand, old chap. We're all more pleased than we can say. God bless ! Of course, with the old man being as he is, we can't exactly kill the fatted calf, but . . .

CHARLES. Don't worry ! I'll consider it killed.

KITTY (*to* CHARLES). Did you know you'd been awarded a medal, post-humorously ? (*She moves above* CHARLES, *then above the settee.*)

CHARLES. Great Scott ! No.

CHETWYND. Must have put up a darn good show, old fellow.

GEORGE. Was in all the papers.

CHARLES (*moving to the armchair down* R.). I must admit I got a shock to find the war has been over two years, and that we had won. (*He sits.*) My last recollection on the subject was that the Allies were just as likely to lose.

(SHELDON *enters up* C.)

TRUSLOVE (*rising and moving down* R.C.). I'm sure Mr Charles wants to see his father.

SHELDON (*easing down* L.C. ; *to* CHETWYND). By your leave, sir. I've just been speaking with Dr Sanderstead. I thought it wise. He says that for a man of Mr Rainier's age, complete recovery can't be expected, but we can hope for some improvement shortly that will enable him to face . . .

CHARLES (*interrupting*). I gather Dr Sanderstead says that my father shouldn't be told about me till he's a good deal better than he is at present.

SHELDON. Aye, 'tis so, Mr Charles.

CHARLES. I suppose after all this time we can both wait a bit longer.

TRUSLOVE. But the problem has a legal as well as a medical side.

(SHELDON *eases up* C.)

Certainly we would wish to spare Mr Rainier any kind of shock, but can we be sure that he himself would wish to be spared—when the alternative is what it is ?

LYDIA. Dr Sanderstead said to me only yesterday that in his present state a shock might kill him.

TRUSLOVE. But we have Mr Charles to think about.

CHARLES. Oh, for heaven's sake, don't bother about me !

TRUSLOVE. Very natural of you to say that, Mr Charles, but there's the question of the Will. None of us should forget we're dealing with an estate of considerable value. What would be your father's wishes if he were to know that you were so—so happily restored to us ?

GEORGE. Good old Truslove.

LYDIA. He's a very sick man, Mr Truslove.

TRUSLOVE. Precisely—and I am sure his desire would be to make certain adjustments necessary for the fair and equal division.

CHARLES. I get your point, Truslove, but I'm not really interested in that side of it.

TRUSLOVE. But it's my duty . . .

CHARLES (*rising*). I don't want to see my father if there's any chance the shock might be bad for him, and I don't give a damn whether I'm in or out of his Will !

CHETWYND (*to* CHARLES). Come, come, old chap. I do understand what Truslove feels. Legally you're—well, I won't say *dead* exactly—but not normally alive. What I mean is, if anything were to happen to the old man—you wouldn't get a look in. Now that's not fair to you, especially as there's plenty in the moneybags for everybody. Good biz. That's why I think Truslove's right.

LYDIA (*easing up* L.). Remember what Dr Sanderstead said. Any shock . . .

CHETWYND. There must be some way of breaking the good news gently.

GEORGE (*rising*). Sheldon ! (*He joins* LYDIA *up* L.)

CHARLES. No, George. Let's drop the matter. I don't suppose there'll be any difficulty about my resuming the income we all had from mother ?

(TRUSLOVE *shakes his head.*)

CHETWYND (*moving in* L.C.). But, good God, man ! You can't live on that.

CHARLES. Why not ?

CHETWYND. But what would you do ? Of course, if you fancied a salaried job in one of the factories . . .

CHARLES. 'Fraid I should hate it. Anyway, I've made up my mind to go to Cambridge.

CHETWYND. Cambridge !

CHARLES. I was going there, you know, when war broke out. Not a bad idea to go on where you left off.

CHETWYND. Well, if anything happens to father, we'll take care of you, old chap. All give you a quarter or something of that sort. (*He looks around at the others.*) Isn't that right ?

LYDIA. But Chet . . .

(GEORGE *sits* LYDIA *on the duet stool.* JILL *and* GEORGE *nod their agreement to* CHETWYND'S *suggestion.* TRUSLOVE *is obviously put out about the whole matter.*)

TRUSLOVE (*moving to* CHARLES). Then I can take that as settled for the moment ? (*He shakes* CHARLES *by the hand.*) If you'll excuse me, I must be going. Let me say again, how glad I am to see you back and looking so well. (*He moves* C.)

CHARLES. Eh ? Oh, thanks.

(TRUSLOVE *nods to the others, then exits up* C., *closing the door behind him.*)

SHELDON (*easing to* R. *of* CHETWYND). I fear that opens up another matter. The moment the servants know, I do not see how we can prevent the story from breaking out.

CHARLES (*sitting in the armchair down* R.). I'm not breaking any local bye-laws by being alive, am I ?

SHELDON. It's not that, Mr Charles.

LYDIA (*rising ; quickly*). Sheldon means that the old gentleman sometimes asks to see a newspaper, and that once the story gets around it might attract a great deal of publicity.

CHARLES (*to* SHELDON). You mean, headlines ?

SHELDON. Aye.

CHARLES. Well, if they think they're going to make headlines out of me, they're damn well mistaken. I just won't see any reporters.

(GEORGE *moves to the armchair down* L. *and sits.*)

SHELDON. I'm afeared that would not do much good.

CHETWYND. It's their job to get the news, old boy, and they usually manage it somehow or other.

GEORGE. Dead on every pin.

(*There is a pause.*)

CHARLES (*to everyone*). Well, what do you all suggest ?

SHELDON. I was thinking, sir, that if somebody were to explain the matter personally on the telephone, giving the facts and using Mr Rainier's state of health as ground for the request . . .

CHETWYND. You mean, get in touch with the editors ?

SHELDON. No, not the editors, sir, the owners. (*To* CHARLES.) Mr Rainier has a large newspaper interest himself, and that makes for certain . . .

CHARLES. Owns a paper, does he ? I never knew that.

JILL. The latest perk, darling. Acquired since your time.

GEORGE. *The Evening Record.*

LYDIA. Chet, you'd better go and start telephoning right away.

CHETWYND (*to* CHARLES). O.K. by you, old man ?

CHARLES. Yes, fine.

CHETWYND (*moving up* C.). Here I go. God bless !

(*He exits up* C., *closing the door behind him.*)

KITTY (*moving to the fireplace*). Can you skate, Uncle Charles ? Rogers—you know, the gardener—says the lake will be frozen thick enough by tomorrow.

(*The door up* C. *is suddenly flung open, and* ELSIE *enters in a state of great excitement.*)

ELSIE (*screaming*). Mr Sheldon ! Mr Sheldon ! (*She moves to* SHELDON *and grasps his arm.*) You've got to come at once. The doctor says you've got to come at once.

SHELDON. All right, all right. Whisht ! (*He moves to the door up* C.) That's no way to go on.

(*He exits, followed by* ELSIE, *who closes the door behind them.*)

LYDIA. Oh dear, I suppose that's another scare. What a good thing, Charles, you didn't go up to the old gentleman.

CHARLES (*noncommittally*). Perhaps.

KITTY (*to* CHARLES). When he feels very bad, he always asks for Sheldon.

(LYDIA *eases to the french windows and stands gazing out over the garden.*)

JILL (*chattering*). What a dreadful tyrant he used to be. (*To* CHARLES.) Remember your birthday when he was away, and mother let you ask anybody you liked to the party ? And when we were in the middle of playing sardines, in walked the old—devil. (*She laughs.*) Every time he opened a door or pulled back a curtain, there was a dirty-faced small boy behind it.

CHARLES. Yes. And young Larry Pringle gave him a hell of a push through those curtains over there, thinking it was me. (*He rises.*) Still the same old curtains. (*He laughs.*) Poor Larry's face when he saw who it really was. By the way, what happened to Larry ?

JILL. He did terribly well in the war. Got rows of medals, ending up with the D.S.O.

(KITTY *sits on the settee,* R. *of* JILL.)

CHARLES. Did he, by Jove ! What's he doing now ?

JILL. Oh, now he's commissionaire outside the Ritz. He's awfully good—does it with a sort of *je ne sais quoi*.

(CHETWYND *enters up* C. *He looks very pleased with himself.*)

CHETWYND (*easing* L.C.). Got straight on to Borrell of the *International Press*—there won't be a word anywhere. Censorship at source. Borrell was puzzled at first, but eventually said he'd pass the word round. God bless !

CHARLES. Oh—thanks.

CHETWYND (*after a pause ; to* CHARLES). Feel like taking a gun out tomorrow, old boy ? We're shooting over at Runners Wood.

CHARLES. Last time I remember any shooting, I was the pheasant. No thanks, Chet, I'm afraid hereafter my sympathies are with the pheasants. (*He moves to the door up* C.)   Do you mind, I'm awfully tired, I'd like to lie down for a bit.

KITTY (*rising quickly*).   Shall I come with you, Uncle Charles ?

LYDIA (*moving to* CHARLES).   But of course, let me show you . . .

CHARLES.   I know my way, thanks.   I'll ferret out Sheldon. He'll fix me up with a room.

(*He exits, closing the door behind him.   There is a pause.*)

CHETWYND (*crossing to the duet stool*).   Well, you never know what's going to happen next !   (*He sits.*)

(KITTY *resumes her seat on the settee.*)

Fancy the old lad turning up.

(LYDIA *moves to the armchair down* R. *and sits.*)

JILL (*suddenly*).   God !   That cigarette case he left me !

LYDIA.   What about it ?

JILL.   I popped it.

GEORGE.   Pity he hates golf like the rest of you.

LYDIA.   I think there's something fishy about Charles.

KITTY.   You've never seen him before, so how can you think anything ?

JILL.   Kitty, please.

(*The light is growing dim as twilight falls.*)

LYDIA.   His mind—how do we know his mind . . . ?

JILL.   Don't be silly, Lydia.   Charles is as sane as I am—though I don't suppose that's saying much.

LYDIA.   I think we were a bit hasty about the money.

CHETWYND.   Lydia !   Please !

LYDIA (*her voice rising*).   How can you make important decisions on the spur of the moment ?

(SHELDON *enters quietly up* C., *and closes the door softly behind him. There is a pause.   His air and the tragic look on his face tell their own story.* JILL, CHETWYND *and* GEORGE *rise.*)

SHELDON.   Mrs Jill—Mr Chetwynd—Mr George—I regret to inform you that Mr Rainier has—passed away.

(LYDIA *starts to cry.*)

CHETWYND (*crossing to* LYDIA).   Poor old boy.   (*To* LYDIA.) Cheer up, old girl.

GEORGE.   Can't say it comes as a surprise.

SHELDON.   May I express my deepest sympathy with you all.

CHETWYND.   Thank you, Sheldon, thank you.   (*To* LYDIA.) Come, my dear.

(LYDIA *rises, and* CHETWYND *starts to lead her to the door up* C.)

JILL (*to* KITTY).　Darling, you stay here.　And later we'll go for a walk and take one of the puppies.

KITTY (*rising*).　What about Uncle Charles ?

LYDIA.　What about him ?

KITTY.　Well, the Will didn't get altered, did it ?　Now you'll have to keep your promise and each give him a bit.

LYDIA.　But surely . . .

KITTY (*quickly*).　You promised.　Uncle Chet promised, didn't he ?　Uncle George—didn't he ?　Didn't he, Sheldon ?

LYDIA.　But he said himself, he didn't want the money.　What would Charles do with a quarter of a million pounds' worth of shares at Cambridge ?

SHELDON.　Don't fuss yourself, Miss Kitty—they've promised—they'll keep their word.　(*He opens the door up* C.)

(LYDIA *exits*.)

CHETWYND.　Of course, of course.

(*He exits, and is followed off by* JILL *and* GEORGE.)

SHELDON.　Poor Mr Rainier.　(*He switches on the lights from the switch by the door up* C., *then moves to the french windows and draws the curtains.*)

KITTY (*moving* C.).　Will you miss him, Sheldon ?

SHELDON.　Aye, very much.

KITTY (*after a pause*).　And somewhere at this moment there must be people wondering where Uncle Charles has gone.　I hope they aren't missing him too much.　I hope they weren't terribly fond of him.

CURTAIN

SCENE 2

SCENE.—*The same.　A day in June, 1922.　Noon.*
The furnishings of the room remain the same, except that the pouffe has now been removed and the pedestal table, on which stands an empty flower vase, is now L. *of the settee.　There is no fire in the grate, and the french windows are open.*

When the CURTAIN *rises,* CHETWYND *is pacing the room.　He seems years older, has lost his florid good humour, and is flurried.　He crosses to the fireplace and rings the bell nervously.　He doesn't wait for the bell to be answered, but moves to the door up* C., *opens it and calls impatiently.*

CHETWYND (*calling*).　Sheldon !　Where the devil are you ? Sheldon !　(*He moves to the fireplace, takes his glass of whisky from the mantelpiece, finishes the drink and places the glass on the table down* R.)

(Sheldon *enters up* c.)

Sheldon (*moving slowly to* c.).   I was speaking on the telephone. Your office said to tell you that they'd found some of Mr Charles' papers after he'd left, and that one of the typing lassies was bringing them down by the next train.

(Chetwynd *grunts*.)

Chetwynd (*after a pause*).   Another bottle of whisky.

Sheldon.   You know the doctor said you were not to have it. What's more, you've not had your lunch.

Chetwynd (*turning away*).   Do as you're told.

Sheldon.   Rogers has been up this morning, Mr Chetwynd.   He was asking for his rise again.

Chetwynd (*irritably*).   Damn the man, he can't have it.   Time for economies, you know that.

Sheldon (*drily*).   Full well I know that.   But Rogers is a good man, and with all these new-fangled improvements, he's had more than twice his proper work of late.   Unless something is done for him, I fear he'll leave.

Chetwynd (*shouting angrily*).   Let him leave !   The man's more trouble than he's worth.

Sheldon.   He's a grand head gardener—grand.   I do not know where we'd be without him.

Chetwynd.   I tell you I won't be dictated to by these people, even if their families *have* been here for generations.   A man's got to make a stand—sack him !   Anyone can be a gardener.

Sheldon.   Don't talk so daft, Mr Chetwynd.   He . . .

Chetwynd.   Do as you're told—sack the man—get rid of him. And bring that whisky.

(Lydia *enters by the french windows.   She carries a bunch of roses. She suffers from a troublesome cough.* Sheldon *eases up* c.)

Lydia (*crossing to the pedestal table* L. *of the settee*).   What are you doing now ?   (*She coughs.*)

Chetwynd.   Sacking Rogers.

Lydia.   Really, Chet, you have a genius for sacking the wrong people.

Sheldon (*moving to the door up* c.).   That's what I say.

(*He exits, closing the door behind him.*)

Chetwynd (*moving to the armchair down* R.).   A man's got to make a stand.   (*He sits.*)   You'll have to do without your blooming roses.

Lydia (*arranging the roses in the vase on the pedestal table*).   Why should I do without them ?   You know I counted on having plenty of money, and being able to entertain properly once your father died and we got Stourton.   You know how I planned . . .

CHETWYND (*interrupting*). Well, it's not my fault your social plans have been upset.

LYDIA. Then whose fault is it ?

(JILL *enters up* C. *She is dressed in the height of fashion. For a moment,* CHETWYND *does not see her.*)

CHETWYND. You know we must economize. Unless a miracle happens, you'll probably find yourself out of Stourton and in a two-roomed cottage.

JILL (*in the doorway up* C.). But, Chet, what's really happened to cause this complete panic ? (*She closes the door.*)

CHETWYND. I can't go into it all now—but don't you worry yourself. I'm sure it'll come out all right.

JILL (*moving to the desk*). I don't want soft soap. I want facts. When father died, you said that British business was heading for the biggest boom in history. That's not quite two years ago. What's happened ? What have you been up to ?

LYDIA (*moving and sitting on the settee*). Speculating.

CHETWYND. Like everyone else, I thought the prices of raw materals would rise. So I bought. Prices fell—everyone made the same mistake.

JILL. So you mean you've gambled away our money ? Good heavens ! We're not bankrupt, are we ? (*She moves to the window up* L.)

CHETWYND (*rising*). Not as bad as that, unless the loans are all called in at once. (*He stands with his back to the fireplace.*) But I'm sure the creditors can be kept quiet somehow. Or the bank will relent.

LYDIA. The bank knows your extravagancies too well. (*She coughs.*)

CHETWYND. Look here, I'm not going to take the blame for everything. You were damn glad to leave all the work to me, so long as you thought everything was going well.

JILL (*moving to the french windows*). So long as we thought you knew what you were up to, my sweet. (*She gazes over the garden.*)

CHETWYND (*moving* C.). Damn it, Jill—what did you ever do but draw dividends and spend 'em on clothes and gigolos ?

JILL (*turning*). Mainly clothes—so far. (*She moves to the arm-chair down* L. *and sits.*)

CHETWYND. While you two either gad about the Adriatic, or your rose gardens, I have all the worry. I haven't had a decent sleep for weeks. The doctor says my blood pressure is so bad that he won't be responsible for me unless I rest. Look at me ! Everyone in the office says I've put on ten years.

JILL. All right, my pet. But what are we going to do ?

CHETWYND. I've had to practically go down on my knees to Charles to see if he'll help us out.

LYDIA. It's all wrong that you've had to. We should never have given him all those shares. And the moment he got them he sold them. (*She coughs.*)

JILL. Something tells me that that may be our salvation. Do you think brother Charles will help us out ?

CHETWYND (*wandering up* C.). He must. He won't let the family down. (*He turns.*) Persuaded him to forget his varsity studies for a couple of weeks and go into the financial situation properly. Didn't want him to do anything with his eyes shut. So he's been up in London in the office. (*He moves to the french windows.*) Only finished this morning. I kept right away. " Let him form his own opinion," I said. Sure to be all right. (*He tries to comfort himself.*) Charles' money back in the firm'll put us on our feet again.

JILL. How do we know he hasn't spent the lot ?

LYDIA. Don't be absurd. What could he have spent it on ? He's been at Cambridge, and he's spent his holidays walking in France. I'll guarantee he's still got every penny.

JILL. I wish I had.

LYDIA. He hasn't had a position to keep up like we have. Look what Stourton costs. (*She coughs.*)

CHETWYND (*moving* C.). Lydia's got the whole county on her visiting list. (*Hastily.*) With one or two exceptions.

LYDIA (*viciously*). I'll get my own back on Her Grace the Duchess of Chelsea, don't you worry.

JILL (*grinning*). What ! You want Pretty Polly here ? Try some old Napoleon, she never can resist it.

CHETWYND. We'll have a libel suit on our hands as well, if she hears you calling her Pretty Polly.

(TRUSLOVE *enters up* C., *and moves to* L. *of* CHETWYND. *He smiles especially at* JILL.)

TRUSLOVE. Good morning, good morning. Mr Charles will be here in a moment. He very kindly gave me a lift. (*He moves to the french windows.*) Lovely day, isn't it ? (*He looks out over the garden.*) And your roses, Mrs Chetwynd ; magnificent this year, magnificent.

JILL (*opening her handbag ; to* TRUSLOVE). I've got something for you. (*She takes out a bundle of cigarette cards and holds them out to* TRUSLOVE.)

TRUSLOVE (*moving to* JILL *and taking the cards*). What's this ? What's this ? (*He examines the cards in great excitement.*) British birds. Never the whole set ?

JILL. Just about. I've smoked myself to a standstill for you.

TRUSLOVE (*looking through the cards*). Most interesting ! Look, a fork-tailed petrel . .

LYDIA. When you've quite finished playing with those cigarette cards, Mr Truslove . . .

TRUSLOVE (*putting the cards in his pocket*). Of course, of course.

(*He moves above* CHETWYND *to* R. *of him.*)   I understand Mr George won't be with us this morning to hear what Mr Charles has to say.

JILL.   George's got sciatica.   Too much golf.

CHETWYND (*moving above the fireplace*).   Where the devil's Sheldon with that drink ?   (*He rings the bell.*)

JILL (*to* TRUSLOVE).   I hear brother Charles has been making a name for himself at Cambridge.

(CHETWYND *stands with his back to the fireplace.*)

TRUSLOVE (*moving to* JILL).   A first-class in the first part of the history tripos—a brilliant achievement in the circumstances.

JILL.   Circumstances ?

TRUSLOVE.   One feels that a man with such a gap in his memory would find it hard to concentrate at all, let alone enough for so stiff an examination.   He's probably got a great scholastic career ahead of him.

(LYDIA *coughs.*)

(*He moves* C.)   Have you made up your mind about selling Stourton, Mr Chetwynd ?

CHETWYND.   All depends what happens at this meeting with Charles.   Damn it all, where is he ?

(ELSIE *enters up* C.   *She is now much more decorous and wears a neat housemaid's uniform.   She carries a tray with a decanter of whisky, and glasses on it.*)

LYDIA.   Whatever are *you* doing here, Elsie ?

ELSIE (*moving* C. ; *nervously*).   I don't know, mum.   Mr Sheldon he says to me, " Elsie," he says, " with all this economizing, you'll probably find yourself parlourmaid tomorrow, so you'd best be making a start. (*The decanter wobbles ominously.*)   Take Mr Chetwynd his poison."

(TRUSLOVE *moves quickly to* ELSIE, *takes the wobbling tray from her and carries it across to* CHETWYND, *who places it on the table down* R.   LYDIA *glares angrily at* ELSIE.)

LYDIA (*controlling herself*).   I see.   Now you may go.

(CHARLES *enters up* C.   *He wears a light grey suit with trousers almost Oxford bags.   He looks sunburnt and well.   He carries a brief-case.* ELSIE *gazes at him for a few moments with god-like devotion, then exits up* C., *closing the door behind her.* TRUSLOVE *eases above the settee.*)

JILL.   Ah !   Here's the great scholar himself.   Hello, darling.

CHARLES (*putting his brief-case on the desk, then moving to* JILL).   I like the new hair style.   (*He kisses her.*)

CHETWYND (*heartily*).   Hello, old man—God bless.

JILL (*to* CHARLES).   You're looking tired.

CHARLES (*lightly*). What an office does to you.

JILL. Well, Chet seems to have landed us all on the rocks pretty successfully.

LYDIA (*bitterly*). With the assistance of a certain undergraduate who thoughtfully added a quarter of a million to Chet's bank loan by demanding cash for his shares.

CHETWYND. Don't go *on* about it, Lydia.

LYDIA. Well, he sold his shares to you, didn't he ? For a quarter of a million pounds.

CHARLES. Chet wanted to buy them—I didn't ask him to.

LYDIA. But he paid you in cash.

CHARLES. I wasn't to know then that Chet had to borrow from the bank to pay me. He wanted the shares.

CHETWYND. Wasn't exactly that I wanted them, old chap. But I had to take 'em. You try dumping sixty thousand on the market and see what happens. I had to take 'em to keep the price firm. Isn't that right, Truslove ?

TRUSLOVE (*a little impatiently*). That was your motive, undoubtedly, Mr Chetwynd. But I think we can hardly blame Mr Charles for . . .

CHARLES. Is it a matter of blaming anybody ? I didn't make it my business to find out all these things before—but I wasn't interested.

LYDIA (*bitterly*). It doesn't cost you anything to admit it now, does it ? (*She coughs.*)

CHARLES (*after a pause*). Wouldn't it be better if I talk to Chet and Truslove alone ?

(LYDIA *has a fit of coughing.*)

CHETWYND. Of course, old boy. (*To* LYDIA.) For God's sake go and get yourself a lozenge and stop that coughing.

(LYDIA *rises.* CHARLES *moves to the desk, opens his brief-case and looks through its contents.*)

JILL (*rising and crossing quickly to* LYDIA). Come on, Lydia, let's leave ourselves in the men's hands. I always feel safer that way

(*She leads* LYDIA *to the door up* C., *which* TRUSLOVE *opens for them.* JILL *and* LYDIA *exit.* TRUSLOVE *closes the door.*)

CHARLES (*replacing the brief-case on the desk*). Damn ! I must have forgotten that report.

CHETWYND. Don't worry, old fellow, it turned up in the office after you'd left. Being sent down by train.

CHARLES (*sitting on the duet stool*). Well, I went into everything, and I'm not very hopeful as a result. It's not only new money that the firm wants, it's new other things.

CHETWYND (*crossing to* CHARLES ; *magnanimously*). You're probably right, old chap. How about a new boss ? Suppose I were to swop around with George on the Board ?

(CHARLES *smiles gently.*)

I know my faults. I'm a fair weather pilot.

CHARLES. I'm afraid it isn't just a matter of changing the pilot. The whole place wants reorganizing, and I can't see George as a new broom.

CHETWYND. Expect you're right—but—the banks won't wait for their money while we mess about reorganizing, will they, Truslove ?

TRUSLOVE (*moving down* R. ; *temporizing*). I think we owe Mr Charles a deep debt of gratitude for devoting so much time to making this enquiry. I'm sure everything he says is very valuable.

CHETWYND. But some of his *cash* would be more valuable still.

CHARLES. In my opinion a loan wouldn't help unless you completely reorganize the firm.

CHETWYND. You mean you won't put up any money ?

CHARLES. No, not just like that.

CHETWYND. Well, I'm damned ! But you mean you'd lend the money if we *did* reorganize ?

(CHARLES *is silent.*)

That's a fair question, isn't it, Truslove ? Let's have a straight yes or no, for God's sake.

CHARLES. Very well, then, I probably would.

CHETWYND (*patting* CHARLES *on the shoulder and smiling*). Fine, old chap. God bless. Now what have I got to do ? Or what's anybody got to do ? *And* who's got to be the feller to do it ?

CHARLES. I'm not a business expert. It's hardly possible for me to suggest a new Board, new factory managers, new heads of departments—in a couple of minutes.

CHETWYND. You think we ought to have new ones—all of them ?

CHARLES. I do.

CHETWYND (*enthusiastically*). Well—all I can say, old chap, is— come and do the job yourself. Lend the money and come and look after it. (*He moves to* TRUSLOVE.) Truslove, arrange a Board meeting and get it fixed up. I'll resign and then . . .

CHARLES (*rising*). But I don't want such a job—I want my work at Cambridge.

CHETWYND. You could go back there afterwards—the reorganizing wouldn't take you more than a few weeks once you got down to it.

CHARLES. I've no desire to get down to it. I don't like business.

CHETWYND. Then it's damnably selfish of you.

CHARLES. But, Chet, I never dreamt of tackling the job myself. (*He breaks down* L.) I don't even know I could do it.

CHETWYND. Well, that sounds like his second " no ". I suppose we'll just have to let the little tick go back to his lesson books.

(KITTY *enters with a rush up* C. *She is now seventeen and correspondingly grown up. She is wearing riding breeches.*)

KITTY (*crossing quickly to* CHARLES). Charles ! They told me you were here. How gorgeous to see you. (*She turns.*) Oh, Uncle Chet, a girl from the office is waiting in the hall.

CHETWYND (*to* CHARLES). Must be your blasted papers.

KITTY. I think she must be new. She's awfully nice. What's her name ? She's a redhead.

CHETWYND. Redhead. Must be Miss Haslett—she's new. (*Cynically*). Doesn't look as though she'll be in this job long. (*He moves to the door up* C.) The sooner we wind up the firm the better.

(*He exits angrily up* C., *slamming the door behind him.*)

CHARLES (*to* TRUSLOVE). I'm sorry. We seem to be wasting your time. (*He crosses to the settee and sits on it at the* R. *end.*)

TRUSLOVE (*moving to* L. *of the settee*). Not at all. The whole situation is most regrettable. You are happy at Cambridge. It must be pleasant and peaceful for you—just what you need. Got comfortable rooms ?

CHARLES. Most comfortable and very peaceful. They overlook the Backs.

KITTY. I suppose you all have mad parties and try and forget there was ever a war.

CHARLES. A lot of the chaps try to forget but it doesn't come off. Very old young men wearing dyed khaki—very strange young men apt to go berserk in the middle of a rag, or start wimpering during a thunderstorm—because of shell shock.

TRUSLOVE. But you've settled down, Mr Charles.

CHARLES (*smiling*). Yes. I'm what's known as a nice quiet reading gentleman.

KITTY. And when you read, do you put a wet towel round your head ?

CHARLES (*shaking his head*). Sorry. I do most of my work in a punt on the river. Or in the orchard at Grantchester.

KITTY. " But Grantchester ! ——

(*She turns to the french windows and gazes out over the garden.*)

—Ah ! Grantchester !
There's peace and holy quiet there.
Great clouds along pacific skies,
And men and women with straight eyes."

TRUSLOVE (*after a pause ; quietly*). Stay up at Cambridge, Mr Charles, and forget the family business. When all's said and done, it's not your responsibility.

CHARLES. No, I don't suppose it is. But . . .

TRUSLOVE (*moving to the door up* C.). Good-bye. Good-bye, Miss Kitty.

(*He exits up* C.)

.

KITTY (*moving to the desk*).   Do you mind if I smoke a cigarette ? (*She takes a cigarette from the box on the desk.*)

CHARLES (*surprised*).   Cigarette ?   Well . . .

KITTY.   I do smoke, you know—most of the girls at Kirby do as soon as they get into the sixth.   (*She picks up the box of matches from the desk.*)   You don't mind, do you ?   (*She lights the cigarette and replaces the matches on the desk.*)

CHARLES.   Not particularly.

KITTY.   I knew you wouldn't.   (*She eases* C.)   You don't give a damn about anything.

CHARLES.   Do they also say damn in the sixth ?

KITTY.   No.   But Jill says that you don't give a damn about anything.

CHARLES.   I see.   Well—go ahead, Miss nineteen twenty-two.

KITTY.   I'll have to stay here and finish it.   (*She puffs at the cigarette and almost chokes.*)   Charles ?

CHARLES.   H'mm ?

KITTY.   Charles—are you—happy ?

CHARLES.   Oh, happy enough.

KITTY.   Charles, (*she moves below the settee*) would you mind if I came to Newnham ?   After you're back at Cambridge.

CHARLES.   Don't see how I could stop you.

KITTY.   Do you think Newnham would be good for me ?

CHARLES.   Another question is—would you be good for Newnham ?

KITTY.   Oh, Uncle Charles !

CHARLES.   I'm not your uncle, Kitty.

KITTY (*sitting on the settee,* L. *of* CHARLES).   Charles, have you ever remembered anything about those years you were lost ?

CHARLES.   Not a thing, properly.

KITTY.   What do you mean—properly ?

CHARLES.   Sometimes a tune—a scent—a name in the newspaper, or a look at something or somebody, will remind me for a second . . .

KITTY (*breathlessly*).   Yes ?

CHARLES.   I try to catch hold of it but before I can—it's gone. (*With an effort.*)   But still—forgetfulness has its points.   I expect you'd rather I forgot about you smoking that cigarette—or don't you mind ?

KITTY.   Perhaps I'm like you—I don't give a damn.   Poor Charles !   Will you write to me, sometimes ?

CHARLES.   Maybe.

KITTY.   Promise.

CHARLES.   All right.   I promise.

(KITTY *flings her arms around* CHARLES' *neck and hugs him.   As she does so,* HELEN *enters up* C.   *She carries a small attaché case.* CHARLES *looks at her for a moment over* KITTY'S *head, then disengages himself and rises.*)

Hello.   Who are you ?

B

KITTY (*rising and easing* L. *of the settee*). You're Miss Haslett, aren't you ? From the office. Suppose I'd better change before lunch, or Aunt Lydia'll be after me.

(*She scampers to the door up* C. *and exits.* HELEN *moves to the desk, places her attaché case on it, opens the case and takes out some papers in a folder.*)

HELEN. . I brought down your papers and the report you left behind, Mr Rainier. (*She moves* C.)

CHARLES (*moving to* R. *of* HELEN). Oh, er—thanks. (*He takes the papers from her.*)

HELEN. I understand there is a typewriter in the library. Perhaps Mr Chetwynd would like me to do some extra copies of it before I catch my train back.

CHARLES. That might be an idea. (*He glances at the report.*) What a depressing document. (*He crosses below* HELEN *to* L.) The sad epitome of a muddle. How long would it take you to copy it ?

HELEN. About half an hour.

CHARLES. Good Lord ! Only that ? It takes me ages to do an address, with two fingers. Is it very difficult to learn to type properly ?

HELEN. Not if you're grimly determined to become efficient in the least possible time.

CHARLES. And you were determined ?

HELEN. Very.

CHARLES (*after a pause*). You've not been with the firm long, have you ?

HELEN. Twelve weeks and four days. (*She pauses.*) Mr Rainier, will you be needing a private secretary ? . .

CHARLES. I ? Whatever for ?

HELEN (*pointing to the report*). Well, with that—muddle, as you say, Mr Rainier, you'll need all the help you can get to save the firm.

CHARLES. Oh. (*He throws the folder on to the desk. Angrily.*) And why should the firm of Rainiers be saved ? What good does it do ? (*He sits on the duet stool.*) Except keep the family going. I'm not sure *that* fills me with great respect.

HELEN (*quietly*). It keeps about three thousand other families going as well.

CHARLES (*angrily*). So you think I should be Atlas and bear three thousand families on my shoulders ?

HELEN. You'd give them security.

CHARLES. Security ! I can't give them security—no one can. Security's an illusion fostered by banks, insurance companies, building societies, and everybody who goes without what he wants today because he thinks he'll enjoy it more tomorrow. Supposing we all find out there is no tomorrow ?

HELEN. So long as we aren't too cold or too hungry until we do find out.

CHARLES (*looking searchingly at her*).   In fact, Miss——

HELEN.   Haslett.   Helen Haslett.

CHARLES.   —you're telling me to come down to post-war earth and provide three thousand families with regular money for fags and beer.

HELEN.   Yes.   I think you're lucky to have the chance.

CHARLES.   You do ?   (*He rises.*)   I suppose I could go back to my lesson books after a while.

HELEN.   Yes.

(*There is a pause.*)

CHARLES.   Maybe you're right.   (*He breaks down* L.)   If it's possible to put Rainiers back on its feet again, perhaps I'd better do it.

HELEN.   Then you *will* need a private secretary.   May I apply for the post ?   At the moment I get thirty-seven and six a week. My typing speed is sixty and my shorthand one hundred and twenty——

(CHARLES *looks sharply at her.*)

—one hundred and ten, and I've had a certain amount of experience in book-keeping.   My French is bad—but improving.

CHARLES (*amused at her exact statements*).   Can you make a good strong cup of tea ?

HELEN (*slightly taken aback*).   I—I think so.

CHARLES.   Then I'll give you a month's trial.

HELEN (*terribly pleased, but trying to conceal it*).   Thank you, Mr Rainier.

(SHELDON *enters up* C.   HELEN *breaks to the fireplace.*)

SHELDON (*moving to* CHARLES).   Mr Charles, will you speak to Mr Chet about sacking Rogers ?

CHARLES.   Sacking Rogers ?

SHELDON.   Aye.   He's a good man, I would not like to see him go.

CHARLES.   I'll see what I can do.

(*There is a pause.*)

SHELDON (*quietly*).   Do not give your money away to them, Mr Charles, unless you can keep an eye on it yourself.

CHARLES.   I'm lending it to them and I'm keeping my eye on it, and Miss Haslett here's going to be my secretary and keep her eye on me.   (*He moves to the door up* C.)   And now I'd better go and find Chet and tell him that the precious firm of Rainiers can hang out the sign of " business as usual."

(*He exits up* C.)

SHELDON (*looking disapprovingly at* HELEN).   So you're going to be his secretary, are you ?   Well, he's no business man.   (*He moves up* C.)

HELEN. I don't agree.

SHELDON (*stopping and turning ; taken aback*). What do you know about him ? Nothing. Mr Charles should lead a quiet life with no violence or strain to upset his poor mind.

HELEN. What's the matter with his mind ?

SHELDON. Shell shock. There were three whole years before he came home . . .

HELEN (*interrupting*). Oh, yes. I know all about his loss of memory. (*She pauses.*) A girl at the office told me. (*She crosses to the desk.*)

SHELDON. Aye, it's just a matter of gossip for the females, but someone should know more. (*Grimly.*) Someone should know what Mr Charles did those many months. I think I'll make it my business to find out.

HELEN (*sitting on the duet stool*). And tell him ? That would be very foolish.

SHELDON (*startled*). Eh ?

HELEN. Do you know anything about amnesia ?

SHELDON. About what ?

HELEN. Loss of memory.

SHELDON. I only know that Mr Charles . . .

HELEN. What's your name ?

SHELDON. Sheldon.

HELEN. You've been here a long time ?

SHELDON. Twenty-five years.

HELEN. Listen, Sheldon. You know that Mr Rainier remembers everything that happened to him *before* the missing three years.

SHELDON. Aye, that's very strange to me.

HELEN. It's simple. It's as though his life were divided into three parts, the first part is his life before he was wounded—the second part is his life between the time he was wounded and the moment in Liverpool when he suddenly remembered his name and identity—and the third part is his life since then. He now has a clear recollection of the first and the third parts, but the second part has completely gone. Do you see ?

SHELDON (*rather stunned*). Aye.

HELEN. During the second part he evidently had no recollection of the first part. They say it's quite a common occurrence.

SHELDON. Is it ? And how . . . ?

HELEN (*rising and moving to* L. *of* SHELDON ; *ignoring the interruption*). The point is, Sheldon, the big doctors declare that it is useless if not *dangerous* to tell the person what has happened to him during the missing years—if, of course, the doctors happen to know. The patient should be left to find out and piece it all together himself.

SHELDON (*suspiciously*). How is it you know all this ?

HELEN. I intended to become Mr Rainier's secretary and I made it my business to find out.

SHELDON. Well !

HELEN. Doctors all agree it would be taking a grave risk to meddle in this.

SHELDON (*easing down* L.). Doctors or no, I intend to find out for mesel' just what Mr Charles was up to.

HELEN. Sheldon . . .

SHELDON. What Mr Charles should know.

HELEN (*moving to the desk*). My advice to you, Sheldon, is to look after your own affairs— (*she pauses as she puts the folder in the attaché case, picks up the case and moves to the door up* C.) and *I* will look after *ours*.

(*She exits up* C.)

SHELDON (*looking after her*). Suffragette !

CURTAIN

ACT II

SCENE 1

SCENE.—*The same. A day in April*, 1925. *Afternoon.*
The furnishings of the room remain the same, but it gives the impression of being shabby and neglected. A pedestal pattern telephone now stands on the desk.

When the CURTAIN *rises*, LYDIA *is seated on the settee. She seems to have acquired a perpetual grudge against life. She looks much older and her cough is much worse. She has a cup of coffee in her hands.* CHETWYND *is seated in the armchair down* R. *He has regained some of his former bombast and seems moderately happy. He is, however, rather shrunken. He has a cup of coffee in his hands.* ELSIE *is standing by the desk, tidying it. She is now very neat and sure of herself in parlourmaid's uniform.*

LYDIA (*placing her cup on the coffee table*). Coffee tastes stale to me. (*She rises, wanders to the window up* L. *and gazes moodily out.*)

ELSIE. I ground it myself, ma'am, just before lunch. Mr Sheldon reminded me, that's why I remembered. He likes his coffee fresh.

CHETWYND (*after sipping his coffee*). It's not so bad. Not so bad at all. Anyway, it's hot, eh, Elsie ? Getting quite grown up these days, aren't you ?

ELSIE (*moving below the coffee table*). I'll be twenty-one next birthday, sir.

CHETWYND. Bless my soul, already ? (*He finishes his coffee.*)

ELSIE. Well, I was tweeny maid for four years, sir. (*She takes* CHETWYND'S *cup from him and places it on the coffee table.*) Then when Mr Sheldon gave the rest of the staff notice, all save cook— that's when you were trying to do things on the cheap—remember ? —he promoted me to house-parlourmaid. And that's three years ago—must be.

CHETWYND. It is indeed. And you like being with us, Elsie ?

ELSIE. Oh, yes, sir. Mr Sheldon is ever such a gentleman. Never a word or a gesture that anyone could object to. (*She picks up the coffee tray.*)

CHETWYND. I'm glad of that.

LYDIA (*turning and moving* C. ; *to* ELSIE). Where did Miss Kitty say she was going ?

ELSIE (*moving to the door up* C.). She didn't say, ma'am, just that she needed some air.

(*She exits, closing the door behind her.*)

CHETWYND.　I bet she does, after all that swotting away at College.

LYDIA (*sitting on the settee*).　Waste of money.　What's she going to do now ?

CHETWYND.　Probably join Jill cruising among the antiquities in the Aegean.

(LYDIA *has a fit of coughing.*)

Glad old Charles could come down for the weekend.　Do him good to get out of London.

LYDIA.　He hasn't been near us for months.　Suppose he's too gay to bother with us poor relations.

CHETWYND.　Charles, gay !　He never leaves the office.　Always looks tired.

(LYDIA *has another fit of coughing.*)

I say, old girl, do take one of your lozenges.　Said to him last time I saw him—all work and no play, old chap, makes Jack a dull boy.

LYDIA.　How original of you.

CHETWYND.　What ?　(*He pauses.*)　Oh !　(*He pauses.*)　He ought to find himself a wife, get himself a proper home with someone to look after him.

LYDIA.　Don't be ridiculous.　Of course Charles mustn't marry. By the way, I wish you'd speak to him over the weekend about increasing the allowance he doles out to us.

CHETWYND.　I don't think I'd . . .

LYDIA.　The firm made a profit last year for the first time. Charles might at least give us a dividend.

CHETWYND.　It's up to him, old girl.　After all, he did pull us through a very tricky moment.　God bless, and we have been able to stay on here at Stourton.

LYDIA.　Only because no one would buy it.

CHETWYND.　I could ask Miss Haslett to put in a word for us.

LYDIA.　Why do you always leave everything to Miss Haslett ? Why don't you ask him yourself ?

CHETWYND.　'Cause brother Charles would say " No ".　Only thing ever is to get round her.

LYDIA.　How you can sit there . . .

(CHARLES *and* HELEN *enter up* C.　CHARLES *is now very much the hard-worked business man.　He wears a black jacket and pin-striped trousers.　He carries a brief-case.　HELEN is self-assured and well-tailored.*)

CHARLES (*moving and putting the brief-case on the desk*).　Always know where to find everyone in this house, summer or winter.

LYDIA.　It's hardly difficult nowadays.　This is the only room that is not shut up.

CHARLES (*moving to* LYDIA).　How are you, Lydia ?　(*He kisses her cheek.*)　How's the cough ?　(*He moves and stands with his back to the fireplace.*)

(HELEN *eases down* C.)

LYDIA. Much the same. Suppose you've had lunch ?

CHETWYND (*rising and moving* L. *of the settee*). Would you like some coffee, Miss Haslett ?

HELEN. I should love some. And do you mind if I make some telephone calls ? I didn't have time this morning at the office.

CHETWYND. Go ahead. The phone's over there on the desk.

(HELEN *moves to the desk*.)

(*To* LYDIA.) Well, suppose we leave Miss Haslett to do her phoning in peace. Don't forget your beano this afternoon.

LYDIA. Of course I'll not forget. I'm just going to dress. (*To* CHARLES.) I'm opening a bazaar at the vicarage, such a nuisance, but I feel it is expected of me.

CHARLES (*taking his wallet from his pocket*). Buy a ticket for me in all the raffles. (*He takes a five-pound note from his wallet and gives it to* LYDIA.)

LYDIA (*taking the note ; pleased*). Charles ! What's your lucky number ?

CHARLES. I don't know—I don't think I've got one.

HELEN. Try seven, it's always brought me luck.

CHETWYND. Aren't you being a bit rash, old boy ? You might find yourself landed with—a bottle of cooking sherry—or a cake, a patchwork quilt or a . . .

HELEN. A doll with eyes that open and shut.

CHETWYND. Quite right.

CHARLES. All very useful.

LYDIA (*rising*). Chet, ring for Sheldon to bring some more coffee.

(*She moves to the door up* C. *and exits*.)

CHARLES (*to* CHETWYND). Don't worry. I will.

CHETWYND (*to* CHARLES). Terribly pleased you could come down this weekend, old chap. God bless !

(CHARLES *moves above the fireplace and rings the bell*.)

CHARLES. Kitty's here, isn't she ?

CHETWYND (*nodding*). Gone out for a walk. (*He moves to the door up* C.) Nice having her here, livens us up a bit.

(*He exits up* C. HELEN *lifts the telephone receiver*.)

HELEN (*into the telephone*). London, please. Tower four-five-five-seven.

CHARLES. Only do the urgent calls. You mustn't miss your train.

HELEN. No, I won't. But I want to get those accounts from Sheldon before I go.

CHARLES. The notes I gave you for the speech as we drove down can wait till Monday.

HELEN. You've a fitting with your tailor eleven-thirty Monday.

CHARLES. God, what a bore ! Why didn't you get him to make a replica of the suit I had last year ?

HELEN. You've got thinner. I can choose your ties, but I doubt if I could model for you.

CHARLES (*sitting on the settee*). So I give in with good grace and allow myself to be respectably dressed for life in the city. The city of meticulous nonsense. (*He idly turns over the pages of " The Tatler".*) All of us meticulous little men attending meticulous meetings, passing meticulous votes of thanks for meticulous behaviour. All wearing neat dark suitings—meticulously cut.

HELEN (*still holding the receiver*). Don't you think it's time you took a holiday, Mr Rainier ?

CHARLES. But I don't need one.

HELEN. Italy would be lovely now—all blossom and blue sky.

CHARLES. I'm sure Mussolini's shouting would get on my nerves.

HELEN. Well, he's made the Italian trains run on time.

(ELSIE *enters up* C.)

ELSIE (*gazing adoringly at* CHARLES). Mr Sheldon says if it's coffee you're wanting, sir, it's coming.

CHARLES. Oh, thank you, Elsie.

(ELSIE *exits up* C.)

(*To* HELEN.) It's unlike Sheldon not to come and look me over.

HELEN. He will—when I've gone.

CHARLES. Still the same old feud.

HELEN (*into the telephone*). Rich and Melrose ? ... Miss Harper, please.

CHARLES. No, I can't get away yet awhile.

HELEN (*into the telephone*). Is it possible for Mr Rich to call and see Mr Rainier at ten forty-five on Monday ? . . . Thank you. (*She replaces the receiver.*)

CHARLES. I think we're in for trouble at the works. (*He rises.*) In fact I think we're in for strikes all over the country and I must be on the spot. (*He moves* L.C.) Phew ! What a white elephant of a place this is. If it was just a bit nearer London, Chet would carve it up into building plots. But as it's only England's green and pleasant land, nobody wants it, nobody can afford it and nobody will pay a decent price for anything that grows on it.

HELEN. There's a nice, solid feeling though, about these old family possessions. Sort of secure.

CHARLES (*breaking to the french windows*). There you go again with your security. (*He gazes over the garden.*) It isn't an old family possession. My father bought it cheap because the other family couldn't afford it.

HELEN. Well, he must have admired the place or he wouldn't have wanted to buy it at any price.

B*

CHARLES. Oh, I don't know. He liked buying things cheap. (*He turns.*) He once bought a shipload of diseased shark-skins because they were cheap and he thought he could make a profit.

HELEN (*laughing*). And did he ? . .

CHARLES. You bet he did.

HELEN. So that's where you get your flair for business ? (*She lifts the telephone reciever.*)

CHARLES. I had business thrust on me—but . . .

HELEN (*into the telephone*). I want Sheffield, please, double-o-two-three-one. (*To* CHARLES.) But what ?

CHARLES (*moving to the door up* C. ; *smiling*). But I should never have kept the firm's head above water without *your* help. I must get out of this black coat.

(*He exits up* C. HELEN *gazes after him, exceedingly pleased.*)

HELEN (*into the telephone*). Hello, is that the Royal ? . . . I want to book a room for Mr Charles Rainier for Tuesday night . . . What ? . . . Yes, one on (*she smiles*) the quiet side as usual . . . Yes, I'll hold on.

(SHELDON *enters up* C. *He carries a tray with coffee for two on it.*)

SHELDON (*coming down to the coffee table*). Here's the coffee.

HELEN (*to* SHELDON). Thank you. (*Into the telephone.*) Oh, that's fine . . . Thank you very much. (*She replaces the receiver.*)

SHELDON. I made it myself.

HELEN. What ?

SHELDON. The coffee. I made it myself.

HELEN (*surprised*). Oh, thank you, Sheldon. (*She moves* C.)

(SHELDON *pours out a cup of coffee.*)

What's the matter ?

SHELDON. Matter ?

HELEN. Well, don't you want to ask me something ? It's not like you to come in here . . .

SHELDON (*tentatively*). I thought I'd see for myself how you were keeping. (*He eases to* L. *of the settee.*)

HELEN (*surprised*). *I'm* very well. (*She crosses below* SHELDON *to the fireplace.*) And you, you're looking younger.

SHELDON. Summer's coming. You'd best sit down and drink this. I wouldn't be surprised if you haven't had a bite to eat.

HELEN (*sitting on the settee*). I had a sandwich.

SHELDON. Sandwich. Tch ! Tch !

HELEN. Sheldon ! I believe you've at last come to the conclusion that I'm the right person to be Mr Charles's secretary.

SHELDON. He doesn't leave you much time to yourself, but aye, you serve him well.

HELEN (*touched*). Thank you, Sheldon. For three years I've been hoping you'd say that. I just feel nothing except nice things are going to happen today.

SHELDON. You'll end by getting the 'flu.

HELEN (*laughing*). Thanks. Could you let me have the estate accounts—you weren't here when I was down last week.

SHELDON. No. I was away on my holiday.

HELEN. Oh ? And where did you go ?

SHELDON (*significantly and defiantly*). Liverpool.

(HELEN *rises abruptly and faces the fireplace. There is a pause.*)

HELEN (*babbling strangely*). There are some really comfortable digs in Liverpool, in Hope Street.

SHELDON. Digs ?

HELEN. Always stayed there even when we were playing Birkenhead or New Brighton.

(SHELDON *looks puzzled.*)

(*She faces the audience.*) You didn't know I was on the stage, did you ? I was song and dance routine, mostly, in musicals, right up to just a few years ago. *Salute the Flag* was the last show I was in. Did quite a lot of impersonations, too. (*She imitates* ELSIE.) " Mr Sheldon says if it's coffee you're wanting, sir, it's coming—Mr Sheldon's ever such a nice gentleman—taught me everything I know."

(*They both laugh.*)

I told you I was crazy today. (*She turns to* SHELDON.) But you'll forget about me and the stage, won't you ?

SHELDON. I can keep a secret better than most.

HELEN (*impulsively*). Oh, Sheldon ! (*She stops abruptly. Quietly.*) Why did you go to Liverpool ?

(SHELDON *looks at her without speaking.*)

Still as stubborn as ever.

(*There is still no reply.*)

Well, did you find anything ?

SHELDON (*shaking his head*). No.

HELEN. You still worry, Sheldon ?

SHELDON (*abruptly*). Aye.

HELEN. Things mightn't be as bad as you think.

(CHARLES *enters up* C. *He has changed into country clothes.* HELEN *breaks down* R. SHELDON *breaks* L.)

CHARLES (*moving* C.). You two look very guilty. What murky secret are you hiding. (*He laughs.*) Still read those detective stories, Sheldon ?

SHELDON. I'll not say I don't.

CHARLES (*to* HELEN). Sheldon's philosophy used to be—
" Sherlock's in Baker Street—all's right with the world ". (*To*
SHELDON.) Remember taking me on that trip to London when I
was eight ? The first place we went to was Baker Street—Sherlock
Holmes' own street. We walked gravely along the pavement, looking up at the tall houses with respectful worship, wondering if our
hero would suddenly appear at a window, dressing-gown, pipe and
all. I don't know which of us was the most excited.

HELEN. I can guess.

SHELDON. Must be twenty years if it's a day, Mr Charles. What a
memory you've got.

CHARLES. Yes, yes, I suppose I have about most things. (*To*
HELEN.) If you've time, could we run over those notes after all ?

(HELEN *moves to the desk, opens the brief-case and takes out some
papers.*)

SHELDON (*moving to the door up* C.). You should not work her
twenty-four hours of the day.

CHARLES. Come now, Sheldon, Miss Haslett has always been
able to stand up for herself.

SHELDON (*chuckling*). Aye—I've noticed that.

(*Still chuckling, he exits up* C.)

HELEN (*moving to* R. *of* CHARLES). Here are the notes. (*She starts
to read them.*) " It is proposed, in addition to the usual dividend of
ten per cent, to issue new shares at forty-five shillings and sixpence
in the proportion of one to five held by existing shareholders."
(*She looks up.*) When I first came, the shares stood at five shillings.
It's pretty marvellous what faith can do.

CHARLES. Faith !

HELEN. Don't you believe in faith ?

CHARLES. Oh yes, but faith is something more passionate, and at
the same time, more tranquil than anything I've ever felt in board
rooms and offices.

HELEN. Where, then, does one look for it ?

CHARLES (*taking the papers from* HELEN). I don't know—I don't
know. (*He glances at the papers, then throws them down on to the
coffee table.*)

(KITTY *enters by the french windows. She wears a coat and a little
fur cap. She has developed into a self-possessed young lady, full of
vitality. She carries a bunch of violets.* CHARLES *turns and stares
at her.*)

KITTY (*moving to* L. *of* CHARLES). Charles, darling ! Here's the
bad penny once again. You're thinner. It's a perfectly heavenly
day. I've walked miles. Oh, hello, Helen. Would you like these

violets ? I've just picked them. (*She holds the violets out to* CHARLES.) Smell.

(CHARLES *takes the violets, sniffs at them, then passes them to* HELEN.)

HELEN (*taking the violets*). Oh, they're lovely. Thank you. How are you ?

KITTY. Fine. And thoroughly windblown. (*She looks around.*) I always thought there was a mirror here ?

HELEN. There's one in the hall.

KITTY. Well, I'll go and peel these off. (*To* CHARLES.) Charles—how do you like my hat ?

CHARLES. Very much—but I've seen it before.

KITTY (*removing her cap and stuffing it in her coat pocket*). Oh, no, you haven't. (*She moves to the door up* C.) It's new.

(*She exits up* C., *closing the door behind her.* CHARLES *stares after her.*)

CHARLES (*staring at the closed door up* C.). Helen . . .

HELEN (*alert*). Yes ?

CHARLES. Haven't we seen that cap before ?

HELEN (*slowly*). I—don't think so.

CHARLES (*turning*). I could have sworn . . . The cap, violets . . . no, it's no use—it's gone. (*He pulls himself together.*) Let me see, what were we doing ?

(KITTY *enters up* C. *She has removed her coat and carries it over her arm.*)

HELEN (*indicating the papers on the coffee table*). Drafting this speech.

KITTY. Oh, Charles, do talk to me for a while.

CHARLES. Of course. (*To* HELEN.) You finish it, you know what's wanted.

(KITTY *moves above the settee, then down* R. HELEN, *her face expressionless, picks up the papers from the coffee table.*)

HELEN. I'll just get those accounts from Sheldon. (*She moves to the desk and replaces the papers in the brief-case.*)

CHARLES. Come and see me before you go.

(HELEN *exits up* C. KITTY *drops her coat on to the armchair down* R.)

KITTY. What are you up to ? (*She moves to the settee and sits at the* R. *end of it.*) It's Saturday afternoon.

CHARLES (*moving to the settee*). Only preparing a speech for a shareholders' meeting. (*He sits on the settee,* L. *of* KITTY.)

KITTY. Do you really have to prepare speeches ? Speaking always seems to come so easily to you.

CHARLES. Just practice. Actually, I loathe speaking in public— always secretly afraid I'm going to break down or stammer or something. Stammering especially. Of course, I never do.

KITTY. I'm so glad you came this week-end. It *is* nice to see you again. I feel so sad really. I've said good-bye to so many people at Cambridge, there seems nobody left in the world but you.

CHARLES (*laughing*). I'm glad I never had the experience of leaving Cambridge knowing it would be for good. First I was leaving for a term—then two terms, and so on.

KITTY. And what now? Don't say you've given it up altogether?

CHARLES. It must have given me up, anyway.

KITTY (*rising*). That's so awful to think of—you fitted Cambridge life somehow. (*She crosses to* R. *of the desk.*)

CHARLES. I fit into the City, too, quite well.

KITTY. No, not really. I wish you'd be yourself—as you were in all those letters you used to write to me.

CHARLES. Now what are you talking about?

KITTY. You. *You.* You're not happy—you're not *real.* But those letters you wrote were real. When you were crushed and hopeless and things had gone wrong all day, you used to sit in your office when everyone had gone home and type them yourself, with all the mistakes.

CHARLES. They weren't so bad, except for the B's.

KITTY. I suppose I'm being sentimental. The little college girl, treasuring letters from an adored hero.

CHARLES (*rising and moving* C.). By the way, how is Roland?

KITTY (*easing to the french windows ; soberly*). Oh, it's all over.

CHARLES. Completely?

KITTY. Yes, he's gone to Russia.

CHARLES. I always thought he was the special one.

KITTY. I had hoped so. But I was never really in love with him, you know.

CHARLES (*moving and sitting on the duet stool*). Well, anyway, you were much too young.

KITTY. No, Charles, I'm not young—not really. Of course you finished it—that night you took us out to dinner.

CHARLES (*surprised*). *I* finished it?

KITTY. I could see you didn't like him. I can't bear to do things you don't want. (*She pauses and crosses in silence to the fireplace.*) Can't you see you've spoilt me for other men?

CHARLES. But, my dear, that's ridiculous.

KITTY (*quietly*). I'm not asking for anything. I'll probably marry someone eventually and be quite happy. But it'll have to be a man whom *you* like fairly well, and who likes you. It's queer how I can talk to you. Though you don't really talk to me. There always seems a brake on. I can hardly believe you wrote me those letters.

CHARLES. To be honest, I don't remember much about them. I suppose you haven't kept any of them?

KITTY. Oh no, never. You thought I was too young to understand, that's why you could write to me like you did. (*She turns and faces the fireplace.*) Of course, I was crazy about you—always have been since that day you caught me stealing the icing here in this study. (*She turns and faces him.*) Remember?

(CHARLES *nods.*)

It might be fun if you loved me now. We'd have a good deal in common. I sometimes wonder why you don't.

CHARLES. In my slow and careful way—I've been wondering that, too—ever since you came through the window in that ridiculous fur cap.

KITTY (*moving to* L. *of the settee ; breathlessly*). Well, just to be curious—why don't you?

CHARLES. I haven't said I don't.

KITTY. Oh, *no !*

CHARLES. Would it be so very incredible?

KITTY. It would be fantastic.

CHARLES. Then it is—fantastic.

KITTY. Darling, you don't mean . . . (*She moves to him.*) You're not saying it just to be kind?

CHARLES. I don't feel a bit kind. (*He rises.*) I feel—well, let's stick to—fantastic.

KITTY. I—I don't know what to say for the moment.

CHARLES (*after a pause*). You don't have to say anything. (*He takes her in his arms and kisses her.*)

KITTY. Oh, Charles, how I love you ! (*She sits on the duet stool and draws him down beside her. Impulsively.*) Let's do wonderful crazy things, just to prove it's not a dream. What shall we do?

CHARLES. Paddle down the Danube in a canoe.

KITTY. And up the Amazon.

CHARLES. And up the Amazon. I'll take a year off—from the firm, the city, the three thousand families and everything else. Let someone else do the work.

KITTY. How soon can we get away? How soon can we be married?

CHARLES. As soon as you like.

KITTY. Oh, darling, you're really looking at me now, for the first time.

CHARLES. What do you mean?

KITTY. You never seemed to—see me before. You never seemed to see anyone—except occasionally when something clicked in your mind. You will stay, darling, won't you? (*She lays a hand on his arm.*) You won't shut yourself away again?

CHARLES. I don't shut myself away—silly.

KITTY (*slowly*). When I came in from the garden just now, something, my cap maybe or something reminded you—but from now on it'll be *me* that reminds you—won't it, Charles, won't it?

(CHARLES *goes to take her in his arms again.*)

(*She puts her hands on his chest, holds him off a little and gazes searchingly into his face.*) You're not really seeing me now, are you, Charles. (*She rises and moves* C. *Brokenly.*) No. Oh, my darling, it's no use. I can't fool myself. I mustn't. I know you so terribly well. I've seen you almost alive—just those few fleeting seconds. But you're not alive for me.

CHARLES. What do you mean ?

KITTY. It's the letters all over again. (*She turns to him.*) I was only the letter-box so to speak—where you posted them to another address.

CHARLES (*rising and moving to her*). Kitty, what mad things are you saying ?

KITTY. They weren't letters to a schoolgirl. They weren't letters to me at all. I can't marry you, Charles dear—that's what it amounts to.

CHARLES. But you've just said you loved me.

KITTY. I do, and you could make me perfectly happy if I were selfish enough not to care.

CHARLES. Kitty ; you know, I really don't know what you mean.

KITTY. Dear Charles, I want you to be happy—to be amused—to do things because you want to, not because you're pushed into them. Darling, I'm so nearly the right one, but nearly isn't enough for a lifetime.

CHARLES. It's a story you've built up around me.

KITTY. No. I've a curious feeling that I remind you of something—someone you may have met or may yet meet—because with that strange memory of yours, the tenses get mixed up—or don't they ?

CHARLES (*taking her in his arms*). What does the past matter ? The present and the future are ours. Please don't go away from me now.

KITTY. One day, darling, all this will clear up. And because I do love you, that's what I want to happen.

CHARLES (*moving* L.). I'm sorry—I seem somehow to have let you down.

KITTY (*with an impulsive step towards him*). Please, Charles, don't say that. (*She turns, moves to* L. *of the settee and stands with her back to him.*) Let's forget about it.

CHARLES. My dear.

KITTY. Yes, Charles, let's forget all about it.

(CHARLES *gives a hopeless gesture, then turns abruptly and exits by the french windows.* KITTY *turns and looks after him.* HELEN *enters up* C.)

HELEN. Where's Charles ?

(KITTY *does not answer.*)

Where's Charles, Kitty ?

(KITTY *turns, rushes to the armchair down* R. *and picks up her coat.*)

KITTY (*with a sob*).   In the garden.

HELEN (*easing* C.).   Why—in the garden ?

KITTY.   Why shouldn't he be ?   Must he ask your permission for everything he does ?

HELEN (*realizing* KITTY *is over-wrought*).   I'm sorry.   I'll wait.

KITTY (*shouting*).   Of course you'll wait.   (*Quietly.*)   Oh, why should I take it out on you ?   I'm sorry, Helen.   (*She moves* L. *of the settee.*)

HELEN.   Is there . . . ?   Are you going out ?

KITTY.   Yes, yes.   I must get away.   Somewhere.   Anywhere.

HELEN (*kindly*).   Well, you'd better put your coat on.   It's going to rain.   (*She takes the coat from* KITTY.)   Here, let me help you.

(*As she helps* KITTY *on with the coat, the sympathy and warmth she exudes overcome* KITTY, *who begins to cry softly.*)

There, now.   Button it up.   And the belt.   Where's that little cap of yours ?   (*She takes it out of the coat pocket.*)   You mustn't cry. You look so very pretty.

KITTY.   I wish I were dead.

HELEN.   Come now.   You'll soon feel better.

KITTY (*flaring*).   Better !   Have *you* ever been with someone— watching them look through you at something—someone far beyond ? How can you possibly understand ?

HELEN.   Understand ?   Me ?   (*She puts the cap on* KITTY'*s head, then stands for a moment gazing at her, holding* KITTY'*s head cupped in her hands.*)

KITTY (*forgetting her own misery*).   What is it ?

HELEN.   Strange.   When I was your age, just twenty, I had a cap like that.   Just like that.

CURTAIN

SCENE 2

SCENE.—*The same.   A day in September, 1932.   Afternoon.*

The small pictures, ornaments, flowers, vases and mantelpiece dress- ing have been removed.   The desk is clear except for the telephone and an ashtray.   The cushions have been removed.   The settee, the armchair down R., *the armchair down* L., *and the desk, are covered with dust sheets.*

When the CURTAIN *rises, all the window curtains are closed and the stage is in darkness.   After a moment,* SHELDON *enters up* C.   *He carries some logs.   He wears an old dressing gown over his suit.   He is followed on by* HARRISON, *a young Cambridge undergraduate, who wears an overcoat and scarf.*

SHELDON (*moving to the french windows*). If Miss Helen had let me know she was coming down, (*he opens the curtains of the french windows, letting in the daylight*) I'd have had the room warmed up a wee bit. (*He crosses to the fireplace, kneels and starts to light the fire.*)

HARRISON (*moving L.C. ; shivering*). H'm. It is a bit clammy. How long has the house been shut up ?

SHELDON. Nearly five years this December. Mr and Mrs Chetwynd died within a year of each other ; and no one's lived here since.

HARRISON. Just—you and the dust-sheets.

SHELDON. Aye—and an occasional mouse.

(HELEN *enters up* C. *She wears a big coat. She is brisk with even greater self-control and assurance.*)

(*He rises. To* HELEN.) You'll freeze. You should have told me . . .

HELEN (*moving* C.). Well, I didn't know myself. I suddenly thought it was a good chance to come and see about the roof as Mr Charles is away for the day.

SHELDON (*collecting the dust-sheet from the armchair down* R.). I guessed as much.

HELEN. Mr Harrison wants to write an article about Stourton— he'll need your help.

SHELDON (*collecting the dust-sheet from the settee*). Journalists ! Ask too many questions.

HARRISON. I'm not really a journalist. I'm still up at Cambridge.

SHELDON (*looking at* HARRISON). Are you now ? What College ?

HARRISON. St Swithin's.

(HELEN *moves to the fireplace.*)

SHELDON (*looking at the fire*). That's better. (*He crosses to the armchair down* L. *and collects the dust-sheet.*) Have a look round and I'll answer your questions when I've got the lassie some tea.

HARRISON. Oh, thanks.

SHELDON (*moving to the french windows*). If you go out of this door, you'll come on to the Yew Gardens—they're famous. (*He opens the french windows.*) Go on—have a look at them.

(HARRISON *evidently does not favour the prospect of going out into the cold.*)

Go on !

(HARRISON *exits reluctantly by the french windows.* SHELDON *closes them after him.*)

Some folk are too young. (*Fretfully.*) The house has been lonely of late. Houses shouldn't be left empty for long. (*He moves to the desk and collects the dust-sheet.*) I was thinking only the other day that I hadn't seen Mr Charles for more than a few minutes at a time in the last seven years.   How is he ?   (*He puts the dust-sheets on the chair* L. *of the door up* C.)

HELEN.   Very well, on the whole.   But he's a truly busy man these days.

SHELDON.   Who isn't ?   Not a body sits quiet to think awhile. Gangsters in all the books.   (*He moves to the window up* L. *and opens the curtains.*)   This Edgar Wallace upstart—rushing aboot with machine-guns and never using their brains at all.

HELEN (*smiling*).   And you ?   Do *you* get any peace now ?

SHELDON (*moving* C.).   Aye, I sit a lot—and think.

HELEN.   Still go to Liverpool—for your holidays ?

SHELDON (*quietly*).   No.

HELEN.   So you took my advice at long last ?

SHELDON.   Maybe.

HELEN (*seriously*).   Or did you solve the mystery of the hidden years ?

SHELDON (*after a pause*).   I decided to leave it to the Lord himself to solve—in His own good time.

HELEN.   The best solution.

SHELDON (*looking at her affectionately*).   And I reckoned Mr Charles was in good hands.

HELEN.   I look after him as best I can.

SHELDON (*after a pause*).   And you ?

HELEN.   Me ?   (*She puts her handbag on the armchair down* R.)

SHELDON.   Aye, you yourself.

HELEN.   I work hard.   (*She takes off her coat and puts it over the back of the armchair down* R.)   The busier Mr Charles grows, the more I work ; the more time I have to spend with him.

SHELDON (*lightly*).   But you like that, I know full well.

HELEN.   You know most things, Sheldon.

SHELDON.   Most things.

(*The telephone rings.*)

(*He moves to the telephone and lifts the receiver.   Into the telephone.*) Hullo . . .   Yes . . .   (*He turns to* HELEN.)   It's for you.   The Brazilian Embassy.

(HELEN *crosses to the desk and takes the receiver from* SHELDON.)

HELEN (*into the telephone*).   Yes . . . ?   Yes . . .   Yes, I'll hang on. (*To* SHELDON.)   You and me—we both hang on—just a couple of family retainers.   Mr and Mrs Chetwynd gone, Jill always away and Kitty happily married and living in Java.

SHELDON.   How is Miss Kitty these days ?

HELEN.   We get letters occasionally.   She's very happy.   That was a nice young man she married.

SHELDON.   Aye.   She was real fond of Mr Charles, was Miss Kitty.

HELEN (*into the telephone*).   Yes, speaking . . .   Good afternoon, your Excellency . . . Thank you for those beautiful carnations . . . The office always knows where I am, and today I'm playing truant . . . A dinner with Mr Rainier ? I'll see what I can do, but it won't be before next week . . . Thank you . . . Good-bye. (*She replaces the receiver.*)

SHELDON. Carnations ?

HELEN (*crossing below* SHELDON *to* L. *of the settee*). Five dozen of the most passionate purple. But the President needn't have bothered. I intended to arrange that dinner anyhow. Rainier bicycles should have captured the Brazilian market years ago.

SHELDON. Well, the fire's burning up. I'll away and make you some tea. (*He moves to the french windows and opens them.*)

HELEN. Can't Elsie get it ?

SHELDON (*calling through the french windows*). Hey, young man, you can come back. (*He turns and moves* C. *To* HELEN.) Elsie just comes up mornings from the village. I do for myself the rest of the time.

HELEN. It's really too lonely for you.

SHELDON (*moving up* C.). I like my own company full well. (*He picks up the dust sheets.*) Mrs Jill still sends me picture postcards from foreign parts. (*He moves to the door up* C.) Some of them cause a wee bit of a stir in the village.

(*He chuckles and exits up* C., *closing the door behind him.* HARRISON *enters by the french windows and closes them behind him.*)

HARRISON. So I can come in ? (*He takes off his overcoat.*) Whose house is this, anyway ? (*He moves to the desk and puts his overcoat on it.*)

HELEN (*moving to the fireplace*). Well, if loyalty and faithfulness stood for possession—I'd say it was Sheldon's.

HARRISON (*moving* C.). What a character !

HELEN. Anyhow, the Yew Gardens are worth seeing.

HARRISON (*shivering*). And I believe they're as warm as this room.

HELEN. I like this room. It's always seemed to me to be the heart of the house. So many things have happened here—so many *will* happen. (*Her mood changes.*) It's lucky for me ; it was in this very room that I literally bullied Mr Rainier into giving me a trial as his secretary.

HARRISON. Lucky for Mr Rainier, *I'd* say. You're about as famous as he is. The power behind the throne. How long have you been with him ?

HELEN. Must be ten years.

HARRISON. Good God ! Haven't you ever thought of leaving him ?

HELEN (*almost startled*). Leave him ! No, I've never thought of doing that. (*She changes the subject and becomes the efficient secretary.*) Now, let me see, when does your article go into print ?

HARRISON. Next month.   Is there any truth in the rumour that
Mr Rainier is going to stand for Parliament ?

HELEN.   That, Mr Harrison, is a leading question.

HARRISON.   I hope he goes into politics.   He talks straight, without the cotton wool.   We all know—from England's point of view—
the outlook is stinking.   What do the high-ups do ?   They baa at
us—instead of saying, " O.K. you chaps, what if the future does
stink, let's put it right ".

HELEN.   Well, all I hope is, that the meeting at Birmingham last
night went off serenely, and that our Mr Rainier didn't tread on too
many trade union corns by talking too straight.

HARRISON (*moving to the duet stool and sitting*).   Someone's got to.
It was a break for me meeting him like that, and his letting me
bother you about the article.

HELEN.   You met him on a train, did you say ?

HARRISON.   Yes.   You know how it sometimes happens in trains ;
you talk openly to perfect strangers because you think you'll never
meet them again.

HELEN.   It's always surprising to me how seldom one does meet
them again.

HARRISON.   I was sitting next to him in a Pullman.   There were
some army types talking about their war experiences—dreadful bores
and they got on to the binges they'd had on Armistice night—in
nineteen-eighteen—and what a filthy wet night it'd been.   Mr
Rainier said they must have been drunk, because there was a fog
that night and . . .

HELEN (*startled*).   He said that ?

HARRISON.   Yes.   And then he went on to tell me about the
Somme—how he partially lost his memory through shell-shock.

HELEN (*surprised*).   He told you that ?   How very strange.   He
never mentions it.

HARRISON (*rising and moving to L. of the settee*).   He didn't really
tell me much, except that there were three missing years before he
came home.

(HELEN *turns and faces the fireplace.*)

But it intrigued me enormously, especially when one realizes what a
well-disciplined mind he has.   Didn't he consult a psycho-analyst
or anyone ?

HELEN (*crossing to L.*).   It's the last thing he'd ever do—go to
anyone professionally and talk about himself.   Anyhow, the advice
he'd have been given would have been—" don't worry, the memory
must be allowed to heal itself, in its own time ".   (*She pauses.*)   You
know, I think you must be one of the very few people he has ever
talked to at all about it.

HARRISON (*easing to the fireplace*).   I felt that, somehow.   I think
what really started him off, apart from the Armistice stuff, was that
we had passed a mountain in the train he recognized.

HELEN. A mountain ?

HARRISON (*turning and warming his hands at the fire*).   Yes, called . . . Oh, damn, I've forgotten and I know it quite well.

HELEN.   Mickle ?

HARRISON (*turning*).   Oh, you know it, too.

HELEN.   I know it very well.

HARRISON.   Actually, I climbed it only this summer.   But I was quite startled at a sort of blinding look of recognition on Mr Rainier's face—which faded almost as quickly as it came.

HELEN.   Did he say anything about it ?

HARRISON (*moving above the settee*).   Nothing really.   But when the look faded he seemed kind of—lonely.   (*He moves* C.)   It sounds silly, but he looked suddenly like a small boy—lost.

(HELEN *moves to the french windows and gazes out over the garden.*)

It was then he told me about his loss of memory.   Towards the end of the journey he became rather quiet, and at Paddington he got up abruptly and left without a word.   So I came right round to you.

HELEN (*turning suddenly*).   Came right round ?

HARRISON (*shamefaced*).   I'm afraid it was rather rushing it.   Yes, it was only today I met him, but you see I go home . . .

HELEN (*moving to* HARRISON).   You mean, Mr Rainier came back —today ?

HARRISON.   Yes, yes, didn't you know ?

HELEN.   Of course not.   I wouldn't be here.   I suppose he's sitting waiting at the office for me.

HARRISON.   I don't think so.   I *did* offer to drop him at his office, but he said he was going—he said—to look for something.

HELEN.   To look for something—how odd.

HARRISON.   He was rather—odd, the last part of the journey.

HELEN (*suddenly, in a flurry*).   I must go—I must go back to London.   (*She crosses quickly to the armchair down* R. *and picks up her coat and handbag.*)   I'm afraid you'll either have to come back by train or come another day and talk to Sheldon.   (*She crosses to* L. *of him.*)

HARRISON (*surprised at her reaction*).   Oh, that's all right.   I'll come with you.   I say, I hope I haven't said anything . . . ?

HELEN (*pulling herself together a little*).   Oh, no.   It's all right. (*There is a strained look in her face.*)   It's that it's being rather a strange day.   Mr Rainier recognizing that mountain, talking to you about his war experiences—he may be a little over-wrought— (*she moves to the door up* C.) he may even . . .

(CHARLES *enters up* C.   *He has gained force and vigour.   He seems revved-up to the fast pace of big business.*)

Charles !

(*Her strained look makes* CHARLES *pause for a second, then he turns to* HARRISON.)

CHARLES. Well, young man, you didn't waste much time. (*He eases to* L. *of* HARRISON.)

(HELEN *breaks down* L.C.)

HARRISON. That's right, sir.
CHARLES (*to* HELEN). You *do* look surprised to see me.
HELEN. Charles, I . . .
CHARLES. Yes ?
HELEN (*controlling herself*). You were supposed to be in Birmingham till this evening. (*She moves and puts her coat and handbag on the chair down* L.) Did anything go wrong ?
CHARLES (*smiling impersonally at her*). Not a thing. (*He crosses to the fireplace.*)
HELEN. How did the meeting go ?
CHARLES. Very well. In fact, there was quite an ovation when I announced the new merger.

(TRUSLOVE *enters up* C.)

TRUSLOVE (*moving* C.). And how's Miss Haslett these days ?
HELEN. Very well, thank you, Mr Truslove. (*She moves in to* L. *of* TRUSLOVE.) And you ? (*She shakes hands with him.*)
TRUSLOVE. Business is bad. Hardly any work in, save Rainiers.
HELEN (*interrupting*). You two don't know each other, do you ? This is John Harrison—Mr Truslove. (*She eases down* L.)
TRUSLOVE (*to* HELEN ; *enthusiastically*). So I've had time to take up ornithology properly at long last. (*To* HARRISON.) Birds much more interesting than humans. Built an aviary in the garden. (*To* HELEN.) Plan to cross a canary with a hawfinch.
HARRISON (*taking his cigarette-case from his pocket*). Will you smoke, sir ?
TRUSLOVE. No, thank you. (*He takes his snuff box from his pocket.*) This is my one little vice. (*He takes a pinch of snuff.*)

(HARRISON *lights a cigarette for himself.*)

CHARLES (*crossing to* HELEN). You do look shattered. There's nothing to worry about. I suddenly developed toothache, so I caught an earlier train down from Birmingham and went to the dentist.
HELEN. Toothache ! Oh, dear, how funny. (*She laughs almost hysterically.*) And *I* thought . . .
CHARLES. Yes, what ?
HELEN. Oh, Charles, I'm sorry. Is it bad ?
CHARLES (*slightly puzzled at her manner*). No, it's all right now. I rang the office and finding you were here, thought I'd follow. Do you think there's anything in my idea of opening Stourton up again ?
HELEN. Stourton ? Needs thinking over carefully.
CHARLES. Thought we might ask Truslove's opinion, that's why I picked him up on the way.

HELEN.   Oh, yes, I wanted to see him, too.   (*She crosses below* CHARLES *to* L. *of* TRUSLOVE.)   Mr Truslove, would you mind coming and having a look at the damage to the roof before the daylight goes ? (*She moves to the door up* C.)

TRUSLOVE.   Of course, of course.

(HARRISON *moves to the door up* C. *and opens it.*)

(*He moves to the door up* C.)   A solicitor has to be surveyor, architect, auctioneer, school-teacher . . .

(*His voice dies away as he and* HELEN *exit up* C.)

HARRISON (*closing the door*).   She's awfully nice, isn't she, and terribly attractive ?

CHARLES (*crossing to the fireplace*).   Helen ?   Attractive ?   I suppose she is.   (*He pauses.*)   How's the article getting along ?

HARRISON (*easing below the desk*).   I think I'm going to find it a bit difficult.

CHARLES.   Get Helen to help you—writes most of my stuff—got the human touch, you know.

HARRISON.   This place must cost an awful lot of money, even when it's shut up.

CHARLES.   It's like some kinds of women, too expensive to cast off. Made any plans for when you go down ?

HARRISON.   No.   The only thing I've seriously thought about is journalism.   I'm mad keen on wireless, but I think it's a better hobby than career.

(SHELDON *enters up* C.   *He carries a tray of tea.*)

CHARLES.   I agree.   Well, I've got a few contacts in Fleet Street.

(SHELDON *carries the tray down* R.C. *and places it on the coffee table.*)

Write to me when you're ready for a job I might be able to do something for you.   (*To* SHELDON.)   That's a welcome sight.   (*To* HARRISON.)   Tea ?

HARRISON.   Not for me, thanks.   I wonder if I could get cracking on the house ?   (*To* SHELDON.)   Could you show me the way to the library ?

SHELDON.   Right across the hall from here, you cannot miss it. (*He pauses.*)   The lighting works.

HARRISON.   Eh ?   Oh, thanks.

(*He moves to the door up* C. *and exits.*)

SHELDON (L. *of the coffee table*).   I've seen you look worse and I've seen you look better than now.

CHARLES (*standing with his back to the fireplace*).   I'm fine.   And you ?   Not fed up with caretaking yet ?

SHELDON.   I am, right fed up.   (*He pours out a cup of tea.*)

CHARLES. What would you say to opening the family mansion again ?

SHELDON. Have you the money ?

CHARLES. I hope so.

SHELDON. Good. You require a better house than that awful wee box in Smith Square. (*He hands* CHARLES *the cup of tea.*) Does the lassie agree ?

CHARLES. I think she will.

SHELDON. But there's one thing and 'tis a delicate subject for myself to mention to you.

CHARLES. And what is this delicate subject ?

SHELDON. It's time you were married.

CHARLES. Indeed ? (*He sips his tea.*)

SHELDON (*firmly*). There are many reasons, Mr Charles. You must think against the future. Then there's now. If you open up Stourton, who's to run it ? You're not capable yourself.

CHARLES. Well, Miss Haslett's pretty good at organizing, isn't she ? (*He drinks his tea and places the cup on the coffee table.*)

SHELDON. Aye, she is that. (*He pauses.*) It's my opinion, and I take this liberty because I've known you since you were a wee laddie, Mr Charles, but I reckon it's Miss Haslett you should marry.

(*There is a pause as* CHARLES *crosses below* SHELDON *to* L.)

CHARLES. It is a liberty on your part, Sheldon. (*He pauses, then turns to face* SHELDON.) Actually, I've had the same idea myself.

SHELDON (*with a sigh of relief*). Well, that's a weight off my mind.

CHARLES. For years I was under the impression that you didn't hold with Miss Haslett.

SHELDON. Even a Scotsman can change his opinion.

CHARLES. But hasn't it occured to you that Miss Haslett might not want to marry me ?

SHELDON (*moving* L.C.). Not want to marry you—don't be so daft. Use your eyes, man. She'll marry you.

CHARLES. I wish I was as sure.

SHELDON. Doesn't she give her whole life to you as it is ?

CHARLES. Ah, but marriage isn't quite the same thing. I'm not an easy proposition.

(HELEN *enters up* C.)

SHELDON. Well, here is the lassie, you can ask her yourself right away.

HELEN (*moving and sitting on the settee*). Ask me what ?

CHARLES (*quickly*). Have some tea. Sheldon is just off to see that Truslove doesn't get lost on the roof.

SHELDON (*surprised*). Roof ? (*He looks from* CHARLES *to* HELEN, *then understanding shows in his face, and he moves to the door up* C.) Aye ! Mr Truslove's a rare one for shutting his eyes to essential affairs. I'll away and put *that* right now.

HELEN (*pouring herself a cup of tea*). I left him making for the right wing.

(SHELDON *exits up* C., *highly elated.*)

(*To* CHARLES.) What did you want to ask me ?

CHARLES (*easing* C.). Er— (*he pauses*) what do you think of young Harrison ?

HELEN. Oh—he seems an intelligent boy.

CHARLES. Sounds as though he makes you feel as ancient as he does me.

HELEN. I don't know about feeling ancient—but I like him anyway. (*She sips her tea.*)

CHARLES. Yes, I do, too. He certainly likes you, informed me you were terribly attractive.

HELEN. Good gracious !

CHARLES. He'll probably go far. Anyway, I hope he goes further than writing articles on my ancestors.

HELEN. You haven't much opinion of your family, have you ?

CHARLES. I never liked any of them except my mother and perhaps Jill.

HELEN. You never mentioned your mother before.

CHARLES (*sitting on the duet stool*). No, I suppose I've never really talked to you much about myself and my family. She died when I was ten. She was a delicate helpless little person. But most women would have been helpless against my father. He loved her no doubt, in his own possessive way. Perhaps a less loving and more thought-ful husband would have sent her to a warm climate for the winter. He would insist on taking her for long walks on January days to blow the cobwebs out of her lungs. It also blew the life out of them. (*He rises and glances out of the window up* L.) Those are the hills where he made her walk. You can see the lines of them against the sky. (*He pauses.*) I came down here today to find you.

HELEN (*breathlessly*). To find—me ?

CHARLES. Yes. Helen, I've been wanting to ask you something for some time. When I heard you'd come down here it seemed the perfect opportunity. (*He pauses.*) You think it's a good idea to open Stourton ?

HELEN (*mechanically*). I think it could be done reasonably easily. Anyway, it should be done. It would be a tremendous help if there was somewhere you could entertain properly.

CHARLES. In that case a hostess would be necessary.

HELEN. An asset, anyway.

CHARLES. Helen.

HELEN. Yes, Charles.

CHARLES. You have become completely essential to me. You know that. You've guided my career unerringly. I should never have made so much money or become what they call " a figure in the city " but for you.   In fact, I have never done anything without asking your advice.

HELEN.   Thank you, Charles.

CHARLES (*moving restlessly up and down* L.C.).   Our affairs seem to have survived the storms of thirty-one, and they look as though they'll more than survive the doldrums of this year.   But as you know, I've come to a big step now.   If I take this opportunity of standing at the by-election and get in, my life from then on will be on a much bigger scale.   (*He gazes out of the french windows.*)   I doubt if I could cope with the politics or the social side alone.   (*He pauses.*) I'm sure I couldn't alone.   (*He pauses.*)

HELEN (*after a pause ; helping him as usual*).   Charles, are you asking me to marry you ?

CHARLES (*turning*).   Yes.

HELEN.   Why are you asking me ?

CHARLES.   You are the only person who really knows me, and who seems interested enough in me personally to take on such a task.

(HELEN *rises, turns and faces the fire.   She realizes now that no love will come into* CHARLES' *proposal.*)

HELEN (*after a pause*).   How much, I wonder, do you know about me ?

CHARLES.   All I want to know.   You're intensely loyal, tremendously ambitious for me—and I'm very fond of you.

HELEN.   I see.

CHARLES.   But before you give me your answer you must realize what it means.   I'm asking you to take on a lot more besides Stourton.   Sheldon, the business, my political career, and all the arrangements and entertaining that go with them.   I'm asking you to take on me.   I know I can't offer you . . .

HELEN (*turning*).   I know you very well, Charles, you don't have to tell me all those things.   I know what you want of me.   And I'm satisfied.

CHARLES (*moving* C.).   Then you will . . . ?

HELEN.   Yes.

CHARLES.   You don't want to think it over ?

HELEN.   No.   I'm quite sure.   (*She moves to him.*)   Let's go and tell Sheldon.   He must be the first to know.

(*There is a pause.   CHARLES kisses her hand.*)

There's just one thing, Charles . . .

CHARLES.   What ?

HELEN.   Could we be married next month ?

CHARLES.   October ?

HELEN.   Yes.

CHARLES (*amused*).   Of course.   What date shall we make it ?

HELEN. The seventh.

CHARLES. The seventh ! (*He pauses.*) Oh, yes, of course, that's your lucky number.

HELEN'S *face is inscrutable.   They move to the door up* C. *as—*

the CURTAIN *falls.*

ACT III

SCENE 1

SCENE.—*The same. A day in August,* 1938. *Evening.*
The room looks considerably brighter and the whole effect is much more attractive. There have been some changes in the furniture. The armchairs from down R. *and* L. *have been removed. A radiogram now stands down* R. *and a high-backed tapestry armchair stands down* L. *The drinks table has been moved to* R. *of the door up* C., *and the chair previously there moved to* L. *of the tallboy. The pedestal table is above the fireplace. A fourth Queen Anne chair stands between the radiogram and the fireplace. There is a standard lamp above the settee and a table lamp on the desk. The pedestal telephone has been replaced by a modern hand microphone type, and the blotter and inkstand have been restored. The clock and vases are back on the mantelpiece and the pictures re-hung. There is a bowl of flowers on the pedestal table, and a vase of flowers on the tallboy. There are new cushions on the settee. A high-backed wing armchair stands* L. *of the settee. The curtains of the window up* L. *are closed. The french windows stand open. All the lights are on with the exception of the table lamp on the desk.*

When the CURTAIN *rises,* ELSIE *is standing* R. *of the desk, looking through a copy of "The Tatler". She has gained a certain confidence through the years. After a few moments,* SHELDON *enters up* C. *The years scarcely seem to have changed him.*

SHELDON (*moving* C.). What are you doing with that *Tatler?*
ELSIE. Well, I heard Pretty Polly say . . .
SHELDON (*sharply*). Elsie !
ELSIE. Well, everyone calls her that—even the Bishop.
SHELDON. Only behind her Grace's back. So you'd best remember your place.
ELSIE. Well, I just heard *her Grace* say there was a photo of Mrs Rainier in this week's, and I've been looking for it.
SHELDON. On the middle page—one of our Mr Beaton's best studies.

(ELSIE *skims through the pages and finds the picture.*)

ELSIE. Oh ! How lovely. Why don't she and Mr Charles have one taken together—they make such a lovely couple.
SHELDON. Unless newly wedded, married couples are not of interest. (*He moves to the coffee table and stacks the cups.*) Hadn't you better see to your bedrooms ?

ELSIE (*placing the paper on the desk*). We've had trouble with the bedrooms. (*She eases* C.) And now Mrs Charles's put her Grace and that young gentleman from the ballet, sharing the same bathroom—it's not going to work out at all.

SHELDON. If Mrs Charles arranged them like that, you can rest assured it will work out.

ELSIE. Cook says too much life goes on here. (*She moves to the door up* C.) She don't hold with it.

SHELDON. She's Welsh. And chapel.

(ELSIE *exits up* C. SHELDON *picks up the coffee tray and moves above the settee.* HARRISON *and* TRUSLOVE *enter up* C. *They are both wearing dinner clothes.* TRUSLOVE *is an old man now and* HARRISON *rather a smart young one.*)

(*To* HARRISON.) Your wireless set's come on again, Mr Harrison.

HARRISON (*crossing to the radiogram*). Oh, fine. It's that music hall programme tonight. (*He switches on the radio.*)

TRUSLOVE (*sitting on the duet stool*). How are you keeping these days, Sheldon ?

SHELDON. Not so bad, thank you, sir.

TRUSLOVE (*to* HARRISON). How are you liking your new work, Harrison ?

(*The tune " Sometimes I'm Happy " comes softly over the radio.*)

HARRISON. It's a bit strange being in a permanent job.

TRUSLOVE. Why did you give up journalism ?

HARRISON. It gave me up, and Mr Rainier suggested that I became his secretary. (*He switches off the radio.*) But I don't know whether I shall manage to hold the job down.

SHELDON (*moving to the door up* C.). You will—Mr Rainier makes a habit of keeping his secretaries a long time.

(*He exits, chuckling.* TRUSLOVE *and* HARRISON *smile.*)

TRUSLOVE. Phew ! I'm glad of a breather from—her Grace. She's a trifle dictatorial.

HARRISON (*standing with his back to the fireplace*). She's been as mild as mild so far this evening.

TRUSLOVE. It was brave of our host to take her on at billiards.

HARRISON. The Duchess is happy so long as she's getting all the attention.

TRUSLOVE. The rest of the house party is arriving tomorrow, I gather.

HARRISON. Yes.

TRUSLOVE. This entertaining ! I suppose you have a lot to do with these famous luncheon parties of Mrs Charles's in London ?

HARRISON. I go to some of them. But Mrs Rainier doesn't need any help.

TRUSLOVE. What exactly is she after ? All this ruthless cele-
brity hunting and entertaining doesn't make a home—and I'm
damned if I know what it does make.

HARRISON. Some people say it's made Rainier's career a really
big one. And from either a Parliamentary point of view or an
industrial one—it could hardly be bigger.

TRUSLOVE. I don't deny she's a good wife for a man of affairs,
but the real point is whether Charles' life ought to be cluttered up
with public matters at all.

HARRISON. What do you mean ?

TRUSLOVE. Always felt there was something special in him. And
I can't help feeling that all this sort of spectacular success must fret a
man with a scholar's mind like his.

HARRISON. If he frets at all, I should say it was about that gap in
his memory.

TRUSLOVE. Good heavens ! Do you mean it still bothers him ?

HARRISON. Oh no, only subconsciously. I don't think for a
minute he realizes it himself.

TRUSLOVE. I always thought that his memory of those years
would come back slowly bit by bit.

HARRISON. Well, nothing of that sort has happened yet.

TRUSLOVE (*rising and breaking down* L.). It's a pity—a great pity.

(HELEN *enters up* C. *She wears a dinner gown and is very self-assured
and charming. She wears a bunch of violets.*)

HELEN (*moving down* C.). Charles and the Duchess not finished
their game yet ?

HARRISON. No. I'll bet she's cheating. (*He moves to the drinks
table.*) Brandy ?

HELEN (*moving and sitting on the settee*). Yes, I think I will.

(HARRISON *pours out a brandy.*)

TRUSLOVE (*sitting in the armchair down* L.). The Duchess is a
little exhausting.

HELEN (*smiling*). And at the same time—very refreshing.

TRUSLOVE. Is it a big house party you're expecting ?

HELEN. Not very. Mostly sporting and dramatic. They're such
single-minded people and a change for Charles.

TRUSLOVE. I know. Take him away from all this talk of war.

HARRISON (*moving with the drink to* HELEN). I don't wonder he
dodges some of your luncheons up in London.

(HELEN *takes a drink.*)

The other day I sat between a Sitwell and one of the Lupinos. (*He
eases to* L. *of the settee.*) It's terribly bad for the digestion.

(*They all laugh.*)

HELEN. One thing about mid-week luncheons—the time's so short, the assortment can be as mixed as you like. (*She sips her drink.*)

TRUSLOVE. Luncheon ! (*He rises suddenly.*) That reminds me —I saw some chickweed in the garden, if you'll . . .

(*He exits by the french windows.*)

HARRISON. What's the matter with him ?
HELEN. Oh, nothing. He's just remembered his beloved birds.

(*They smile.*)

HARRISON (*looking adoringly at* HELEN). I love your dress. You look—er—it suits you very well.
HELEN. Oh ! Yes, I think this colour does suit me (*She pauses.*)

(HARRISON *continues to gaze at her.*)

Now, tell me, did you like my secret garden ?
HARRISON (*after a pause ; pulling himself together*). I've been wanting to tell you—just how much. It's perfectly lovely. You don't show it to many people, do you ?
HELEN. Well, no, I don't.
HARRISON (*slightly intense*). Why did you let me see it ?
HELEN (*lightly*). Well—I thought you'd like it. I'm very proud of it. I made it myself out of the gardener's rubbish heap.
HARRISON. What does Mr Rainier think of it ?
HELEN (*placing her glass on the coffee table*). Charles never looks at it. Hasn't time. (*She pauses, rises and moves to the fireplace.*) Sometimes—I do wish I'd find him sitting—quietly—alone—like men you sometimes see outside their cottages in the country—at peace. He never is, you know.
HARRISON. Why do you think he's never at peace ?
HELEN. It's hard for anyone to feel at peace these days. Don't you think so ?
HARRISON. What about the men you sometimes see outside their cottages in the country ?
HELEN (*with a change of tone*). They're probably not at peace at all—just too old and tired to worry about things any more. Not like Charles.
HARRISON. Charles ! Charles ! Always Charles ! (*He breaks to* L.C. *and turns.*) I wonder if he realizes just how much you do for him.

(HELEN *turns and faces the fireplace. Her Grace the* DUCHESS OF CHELSEA *enters up* C. *She is aged seventy. She has a prominent hooked nose. She carries a billiards cue and is smoking a cigar. She does not carry a handbag.*)

DUCHESS (*as she enters*).   Dashing off in the middle of a game of snooker.   Never heard of such a thing.   (*She moves* C.)   Ah ! Here you are.   (*To* HELEN.)   Your husband's called off to the telephone. Hate being left alone.   Quite likely to cheat.   (*She thrusts the cue at* HARRISON.)   Here !

(HARRISON *takes the cue from her and leans it against the* L. *side of the desk.*)

HELEN (*turning*).   Why, Polly !

DUCHESS (*stooping*).   Polly !   (*She pauses.*)   Where did you hear that ?

HELEN (*chattily*).   Why, I think it's a charming nickname.   Suits you beautifully.   Pretty Poll—you know.

DUCHESS (*aside to* HARRISON).   H'mm !   Always hoped one day somebody'd have the nerve to call me it to me face.   (*To* HELEN.) Don't know why I come to this house to be insulted.

HELEN (*moving to the drinks table*).   You come to see me.

DUCHESS (*grinning*).   I do not.   I come for the food and the drink. Reminds me.   Want some brandy.   (*To* HARRISON.)   Best brandy in the county here.   (*She turns to* HELEN.)

(HELEN *holds up the bottle of Old Napoleon Brandy.*)

That'll do.   (*To* HARRISON.)   Now, young man, (*she indicates the armchair* L. *of the settee*) I'll have that chair moved away from the light.

(HELEN *pours out a brandy.*)

I may be seventy, but I'm damned if I like looking it.

HARRISON (*moving the armchair to* C.).   Here you are, Duchess.

DUCHESS (*looking at* HARRISON'S *hands*).   Good hands.   Ride ?

HARRISON.   No, Duchess.   Only type.

DUCHESS (*to* HELEN).   Mind my cigar ?

HELEN (*unconcerned*).   Of course not.

DUCHESS.   Pinched it off your husband.   (*She sits in the armchair* C.)   Excellent dinner.

HARRISON (*moving to the desk*).   Yes, marvellous.   (*He perches himself on the edge of the desk.*)

DUCHESS (*nodding towards* HELEN).   Born hostess—as good as an American—much too good for England.

(HELEN *moves with the drink to* R. *of the* DUCHESS.)

(*She grins up at* HELEN.)   Who's that husband of yours talking to ?

HELEN.   I don't know.

DUCHESS (*taking the drink from* HELEN).   You never do seem to know what your husband's up to.   Last time I was here he'd gone to India and you didn't seem to know.

HELEN.   That's the secret of our happy marriage.

C

DUCHESS. Think so ? I kept Archie on a short curb *and* he liked it. (*She sips her drink.*)

HELEN (*moving to the fireplace*). Well, it suits us. Nearly six years married and not a single quarrel. We'll be qualifying for the Dunmow Flitch.

DUCHESS. Ah ha ! Wait until one of those new platinum blondes comes along.

HELEN. I'll cope with her. But you should have seen the girl he nearly married when I was his secretary. Did you know I was his secretary ?

(*The* DUCHESS *nods.*)

She was prettier than I was and much younger. Kitty ! She married somebody else in a rubber plantation. I can't think why—I mean—why in a rubber plantation.

DUCHESS. Why didn't Charles marry her ?

HELEN. I—don't know.

DUCHESS. Were you in love with him then ?

HELEN. Ever since the moment I set eyes on him. Oh, I admit I was designing about it all. (*To* HARRISON.) I wonder if there's any fresh news on your precious radio. (*She moves to the radiogram.*) Hitler was making another speech today. (*She switches on the radio.*)

HARRISON. Just words, nothing but violent words.

DUCHESS. Better than violent actions, anyway.

HELEN. I'm not so sure of that—as I used to be.

(*The tune " These Foolish Things " comes softly over the radio.*)

I mean, when you're waiting for something to happen and rather dreading it, anything's better than the suspense.

DUCHESS. What do you mean ?

HELEN (*embarrassed*). Oh, nothing. (*She switches off the radio.*)

DUCHESS. You should be wearing one of the famous Stourton roses.

HARRISON (*rising and breaking down* L.). She never wears anything but violets.

DUCHESS. Neither she does. (*To* HELEN.) Must admit they suit you—colour of your eyes. That husband of yours evidently thinks so, too.

HELEN (*moving to the fireplace ; quietly*). Charles hasn't the time. I pick them or buy them myself.

DUCHESS. Buys them herself ! That's the trouble with Englishmen—no approach.

(HELEN *is about to protest when* CHARLES *enters up* C. *He seems older and more settled. If one looks closely, a certain strained look can be seen in his eyes. He wears dinner clothes.*)

(*To* CHARLES.) Just been talking about you.

CHARLES (*crossing to the fireplace*). Nice things—I hope. (*He stands beside and below* HELEN.)

DUCHESS. Doubt if anyone'd dare say anything really nasty, with that wife of yours about. Quite fond of you.

CHARLES. I'm utterly devoted to her.

DUCHESS. Charming. Charming. (*She suddenly turns in her chair and looks directly at them.*) Are you happy? The pair of you?

(*There is an almost imperceptible pause.*)

HELEN. Of course we're happy.

DUCHESS. Umph!

CHARLES (*to the* DUCHESS). Shall we finish our game?

DUCHESS. Don't think so. Not playing well enough.

(CHARLES *moves to the radiogram and switches on the radio.*)

HELEN. Let's have a rubber of bridge.

DUCHESS (*rising and fussing around*). Left my handbag somewhere. Must have my bag. (*She hands her glass to* HARRISON.) Can't play bridge without my bag. Now where did I leave it?

HELEN. In the dining-room?

(*The tune " These Foolish Things " comes softly over the radio.* CHARLES *switches it off.*)

DUCHESS (*remembering*). Billiards room. On one of the stags' heads.

(HARRISON *moves to the door up* C.)

No, no, must go myself. (*She moves to the door up* C.) Know which one when I see it. Reminded me of poor Archie.

(*She exits up* C. HELEN *smiles at* HARRISON, *then moves to the door up* C. *and exits.* HARRISON *moves to the drinks table, puts the glass on it, then moves above the fireplace and rings the bell.*)

HARRISON (R. *of the settee*). Doesn't she look lovely tonight?

CHARLES. Who, the Duchess?

HARRISON. No. Helen.

CHARLES. Yes, very. (*He looks at* HARRISON, *then smiles.*) You're awfully fond of her, aren't you?

HARRISON. Yes, I am.

CHARLES (*crossing to the french windows ; gaily*). Our marriage was a merger that worked out very well. She turned a tired business man into a thumping success. (*He gazes out over the garden.*)

HARRISON. That's one good reason for getting married.

CHARLES. Can you think of a better?

HARRISON (*moving to* C.). There's generally considered to be one very much better.

c*

CHARLES (*not hearing*). She's everything a man like me could wish for in a wife—always provided—he's completely satisfied to be a man like me.

HARRISON. And aren't you ?

CHARLES (*simply*). Sometimes I wonder what sort of man I am.

(SHELDON *enters up* C.)

HARRISON. Could you bring the bridge table, please, Sheldon ?

SHELDON. Aye, I will, sir.

(*He exits up* C.)

HARRISON (*moving to* R. *of* CHARLES). Mr Rainier, can't you do any more about this crisis ? Can't you make people see ? Make 'em understand that war isn't just a threat any longer.

CHARLES (*turning*). Why do you ask ?

HARRISON. You say " a man like you ". You have such drive, such . . .

CHARLES (*crossing to the fireplace ; distantly*). I could do a lot—but the inner strength the real faith is something needed to carry through a thing as big as this. And I don't seem to have that strength. Without it, there's a bleakness that makes men like me turn away at the final count. (*In a lighter tone.*) It's bulldogs that are needed—happy fighting bulldogs.

(HELEN *enters up* C.)

HELEN (*to* HARRISON). Oh, John, go and fetch Mr Truslove in from the garden. He'll catch a chill out there.

(HARRISON *exits by the french windows.* HELEN *moves to the desk, switches on the table lamp and sits on the duet stool.*)

(*To* CHARLES.) I'm sorry about the weekend. (*She takes four bridge score pads, two packs of cards and some pencils from the desk drawer.*) I think you'd much rather have had it quiet with all this trouble brewing. (*She puts the pads, cards and pencils on the desk.*)

CHARLES. Oh, I don't mind. (*He smiles at her.*) Tired ?

HELEN. I am, a little. It's this strange tension in the air.

CHARLES (*moving to the drinks table*). Have a brandy ?

HELEN. I've already had one.

CHARLES (*pouring out a brandy*). Then another ?

HELEN. No, I don't think so.

CHARLES. One more won't do you any harm.

HELEN. Really, Charles !

CHARLES (*moving with the drink to* HELEN ; *charmingly*). Just this small one.

(HELEN *smiles and takes the glass.*)

Before I came down today, I went and inspected the new vaults at the office.

HELEN.   Vaults ?   I didn't know you'd built any—or does one say—burrowed any ?

CHARLES.   New storage vaults, but actually I had another thought in mind.   Entirely at my own expense, I've had the whole place made bombproof.

HELEN.   Bombproof ?   (*She sips her drink.*)

CHARLES (*breaking to the french windows*).   And there's comfort as well as safety—there's an independent heating plant, because it's no good saving people from bombs, just to have them die of influenza. And another reason—the greatest man of the twentieth century may have to be born in a place like that, so let's make it as decent as we can for him.   A steel and concrete manger, sixty feet below ground —that's why I've kept it a bit secret, because you couldn't expect the investing public to swallow *that*.

HELEN (*rising and moving to the fireplace*).   You're very nice, Charles.   (*She puts her glass on the coffee table.*)

CHARLES.   " Och !   I was always fanciful ", as Sheldon says.

(SHELDON *enters up* C.   *He carries a card table.*   CHARLES *helps him to set it up below the duet stool.*)

HELEN.   In case I don't have another word with you, I've put the new Beverley Nichols beside your bed.   Would you mind glancing through it ?   He's coming for the weekend.

CHARLES.   All right.   I won't let you down.

(TRUSLOVE *and* HARRISON *enter by the french windows.*   TRUSLOVE *carries a bunch of chickweed.*   HARRISON *moves to the desk.*)

TRUSLOVE (*crossing down* R.).   A game of bridge.   How very nice. But surely you have a foursome without me ?

HELEN.   Charles never plays these days.   (*To* CHARLES.)   What will you do, Charles ?

(CHARLES *gets the chair from* L. *and puts it* L. *of the card table, then eases down* L.   SHELDON *gets the chair from up* R. *and puts it below the card table.*   HARRISON *gets the pads, cards and pencils from the desk and puts them on the card table.*)

CHARLES.   I'm waiting for a call to come through from Washington, and then, if you'll all excuse me, I think I'll have an early night.

TRUSLOVE.   Good idea.   Good idea.   (*He puts the chickweed carefully on the mantelpiece.*)

(*The* DUCHESS *enters up* C., *waving her handbag.*)

DUCHESS (*moving above the settee ; to* HELEN).   Shall we challenge the men ?

HARRISON (*moving below the card table to* C.).   It's a little one-sided —both you and Helen could beat Culbertson at his own game.

(SHELDON *gets the chair from up* L. *and places it* R. *of the card table, then exits up* C.)

TRUSLOVE (*moving and sitting* R. *of the card table*). I don't mind—don't mind at all. (*He shuffles the cards. To* HARRISON.) What convention do you play ?

HARRISON (*moving* L. *of the card table*). Under the watchful eye of Helen—the one club.

HELEN (*moving and sitting below the card table ; laughing*). But you'll be able to tell by the agonized look on his face.

(HARRISON *sits* L. *of the card table.*)

DUCHESS (*putting her bag on the settee*). Damn fool convention—don't like it, don't like it at all. (*She moves and sits on the duet stool above the card table.*)

HELEN. You'll have to play it with me all the same.

TRUSLOVE. Dear ! Dear ! (*He spreads the cards on the table.*)

DUCHESS. Maybe I will.

(*They all cut a card for deal.* CHARLES *sits in the armchair down* L.)

TRUSLOVE. Yours, Mrs Charles. (*He shuffles again.*)

HARRISON. I wonder if Hitler plays bridge ? (*He cuts the cards for* HELEN.)

(HELEN *deals. The* DUCHESS *shuffles the second pack.*)

TRUSLOVE. I shouldn't think so. No finesse !

HARRISON (*rising suddenly*). Gosh ! We've missed that music hall programme. (*He crosses to the radiogram and switches on the radio.*)

DUCHESS. Music hall ? What do you mean ?

HARRISON. It's a series. Each week they take excerpts from some old music hall show. (*He looks at his watch.*) It must be in the middle of it now.

HELEN. John is a great radio fan.

(*The tune " Land of Hope and Glory " comes softly over the radio.*)

(*To* HARRISON.) What are they doing tonight ?

HARRISON. It's a show I don't know. *Salute The Flag*, or something.

DUCHESS. *Salute The Flag !* Now that was a show ! Saw it first at the Metropolitan—Edgware Road.

HARRISON. Surely you didn't go there ?

DUCHESS. You bet we did. As far back as the nineties. Me and Archie. We'd roar with the best of 'em.

HARRISON. Music hall must have been fun in those days.

DUCHESS. It was fun, even in nineteen-seventeen. *Salute The Flag*—a real flag-waving revue. All about the Boer War.

CHARLES (*suddenly*).   Oh no, the Great War.   Wipers and all . . .
DUCHESS.   What ?   Oh.

(*There is a pause.   " Land of Hope and Glory " finishes.*)

HELEN.   Turn the music off, John.   It's distracting.
ANNOUNCER (*speaking through the radio*).   And here is a song you
all know.   In the original production of *Salute The Flag*, it was sung
by a male chorus led by a pretty girl in a tattered uniform against a
backcloth depicting the ruins of Ypres and the mud of Flanders.

(*The tune of " Tipperary " comes over the radio.*)

HELEN.   John !   You're holding up the game.

(HARRISON *switches off the radio, crosses to his place at the card table,
and sits.   They all arrange their cards.*)

DUCHESS.   I remember that show.   There were some very funny
turns in it, apart from the flag-waving.
HARRISON.   They re-broadcast the programme three-thirty Tuesday.   You should listen-in.
DUCHESS.   I suppose they only do a potted version of the original
show ?
HARRISON.   Yes.   Generally the best scenes and the most popular
songs.
HELEN.   One club.

(CHARLES *rises, crosses slowly to the radiogram and switches on the
radio.*)

TRUSLOVE.   Two clubs.

(HARRISON *looks a bit perplexed.*)

DUCHESS.   Two hearts.
HARRISON.   No bid.
HELEN (*watching* CHARLES ; *unthinkingly*).   No bid.
TRUSLOVE.   Three clubs.   It's up to you, Duchess.
DUCHESS.   What !   Surely not ?   Helen.   No bid ?   Helen can't
have passed.

(*The last verse of the tune of " Tipperary " comes over the radio.*)

HELEN (*starting*).   Oh, yes, I'm sorry, Polly, I think I have.
DUCHESS.   But it's your convention, not mine.   I only gave that
to you . . .
HARRISON.   I'm sorry, Helen.   The radio—is confusing you.
HELEN.   Of course not.   (*She laughs slightly hysterically.*)   What
sort of convention is this, anyway ?   A post-mortem before the cards
are even played ?

(*They all laugh.*)

DUCHESS.   All right, it's yours, Mr Truslove.   (*She leads a card.*)

HARRISON (*putting his cards down*). Perhaps I should have put you up. But everybody bidding clubs got me sort of confused.

TRUSLOVE. That's quite all right, my boy.

DUCHESS (*looking at* HARRISON'S *cards*). Damn well should have put him up. There's a grand slam there.

TRUSLOVE. Hardly that, your Grace. But thank you, partner, thank you very much indeed.

(" *Tipperary* " *finishes.* HARRISON *rises and moves to* CHARLES. TRUSLOVE *starts to play the hand.*)

ANNOUNCER (*speaking through the radio*). We now enter the Colonel's hut. The Colonel is a fine upstanding gentleman with a pair of magnificent moustachios.

CHARLES (*to* HARRISON). Ah ! But he's a German in disguise.

ANNOUNCER. Ah ! But wait—he is a German in disguise. He's copying a stolen Treaty instead of leading his men into battle. His absence is losing the day. But what is this ?

(*An exaggerated knock sounds through the radio.*)

A knock at the door. A very loud knock.

CHARLES (*reacting*). A very nervous young subaltern enters.

HARRISON. You remember a lot of the show, sir.

CHARLES. W-what ?

HARRISON. You've seen the show, sir ?

(HELEN, *distracted from the game, looks across at* CHARLES.)

ANNOUNCER. A young subaltern enters.

TRUSLOVE (*to* HELEN). Your play, Mrs Charles. Mrs Charles !

HELEN (*giving her attention to the game*). Oh, I'm sorry. (*She plays a card.*)

ANNOUNCER. He is a very young subaltern and very nervous. The Colonel's indifference is too much for him.

SUBALTERN (*speaking through the radio ; with a terrible stammer*). The enemy are attacking, sir. G-g-g-give the o-o-order to advance or if you d-d-d-d-don't, sir, then b-b-by g-g-g-gad I w-w-w-will myself.

ANNOUNCER. And with suitable gesture he turns on his heel and makes for the door.

(*The tune of " A Policeman's Holiday " comes over the radio.*)

CHARLES (*quietly*). But the door knob comes off in his hand.

(HELEN *again looks across at* CHARLES.)

ANNOUNCER. But the door knob comes off in his hand.

(CHARLES *abruptly switches off the radio. The game of bridge has come to a standstill.*)

DUCHESS. Yours, Helen. Helen !

HELEN (*making an effort*). Oh, is it my play ? (*She hurriedly plays a card.*)

DUCHESS. That's all right. But it *was* my trick.

TRUSLOVE (*laying down his remaining cards*). The rest are mine, I think.

(*The others throw their remaining cards in.*)

CHARLES. God, that stammer !

(HELEN *rises.*)

They kept it in and the door knob coming off as well.

DUCHESS. Door knob ? Don't remember any door knob.

CHARLES. It wasn't always there.

HARRISON. Strange you should remember so much of the show. When did you see it ?

CHARLES. It's more than that, more than just *seeing* it before. I . . .

HARRISON. What's happened ? You look . . .

CHARLES (*sharply*). How do I look ?

(SHELDON *enters up* C. *He carries a syphon of soda.*)

HARRISON (*carefully*). You look as you did when I first met you—staring at that mountain through the train window that day. There was all that talk of Armistice.

(SHELDON *moves to the drinks table.*)

CHARLES. Armistice. (*He pauses. Loudly.*) Armistice Day !

(*The* DUCHESS *and* TRUSLOVE *rise.* HELEN *eases* C. SHELDON *puts the syphon on the drinks table.*)

(*Quietly.*) I was in hospital—that first Armistice Day—the first one of all. The real one. Oh yes, I remember. It was at Melbury.

DUCHESS. Melbury. What were you doing there ?

CHARLES (*crossing quickly to the french windows*). I think I'll go to Melbury.

HELEN (*staring at* CHARLES ; *quietly*). John, go with him.

HARRISON (*crossing to* CHARLES). Of course. I'll get the car out. Hanson will have gone to bed.

CHARLES. Do you know the way ?

HARRISON. Through Stepney and Stratford, isn't it ?

CHARLES. I don't know. I've never been there since the morning I left.

HARRISON. You remember it was morning ?

CHARLES. Did I say morning ? If only I could *see* it.

HARRISON. You won't see much tonight, I'm afraid.

CHARLES. I didn't last time—because of the fog. (*He tries desperately to hold on to this much of his memory.*) Oh, God, that's something else—something else . . .

HARRISON. Shall Helen come, too ?
CHARLES (*blankly*). Helen ?

(HELEN *motions* HARRISON *to go, and moves to the fireplace.* HARRISON *ushers* CHARLES *off by the french windows.*)

DUCHESS. Hospital ? Melbury ? Don't remember a hospital there. Know the place quite well.
SHELDON. They'll find no ordinary hospital at Melbury, Your Grace.
DUCHESS. That's what I thought.
SHELDON. There's still—just the asylum.

CURTAIN

SCENE 2

SCENE 2.—*The same. Later the same night.*
When the CURTAIN *rises, it is* 3 a.m. *The card table has been removed and the three chairs returned to their places. The french windows are closed and the curtains drawn. The fire has been lit. The room is in darkness except for the desk lamp, which is lit.* HELEN *sits on the settee. She wears a white or pale-coloured dressing-gown. After a few moments,* SHELDON *enters up* C., *does not see* HELEN, *and moves to the desk to switch off the light.*

HELEN. Don't turn the light off, Sheldon.
SHELDON (*startled*). Mrs Charles ! (*He moves* C.) Whatever are you doing down here at this hour ? It's not like you to be . . .
HELEN. To be doing anything—so unusual ?
SHELDON. Mebbe.
HELEN (*slightly hysterical*). Of course not. Mrs Rainier rises at nine-thirty regularly—Mrs Rainier attends every function properly attired and equipped—Mrs Rainier wears the Rainier Emerald with faultless distinction—in fact Mrs Rainier is the perfect automaton.
SHELDON (*moving* L. *of the settee*). Och, lassie, away with you to your bed.
HELEN (*rising and crossing to* C.). Don't cosset me or I shall cry like a child. I couldn't sleep. The house is so big and lonely at this time of night. And this room—well, it's the one corner that's friendly.
SHELDON. Mr Charles going off to Melbury's upset you.
HELEN (*unconvincingly*). No, it hasn't.
SHELDON. Are you worrying Mr Charles has gone off to look for someone ?
HELEN. Maybe. Oh, I don't know.
SHELDON. You must not worry yourself. There is no need.

HELEN. No need ! (*She takes a step towards* SHELDON. *Suddenly.*) How much do you know, Sheldon ? (*She pauses.*) So you did find a clue in Liverpool, after all ?

SHELDON. Not in Liverpool. But at Melbury. It was a hospital for shell-shock cases during the war. Then I happened on a publican called Biffer Briggs—he owned a wee pub called the *Owl* nearby.

(HELEN *gazes at him astonished.*)

He was a grand talker, and gave me much information. He talked of a lass, such as I've known but one. There could be no mistaking his description. From that moment I knew the Lord required no assistance from me in dealing with the problem. I've just bided my time.

HELEN. And you've never spoken about it.

SHELDON. There are some things best left unsaid.

HELEN. So Mr Charles won't find the person he's looking for in Melbury ?

SHELDON. No.

HELEN. Do you think he ever will ?

SHELDON. I don't know.

HELEN (*in agony*). And if he does find her—suppose it's not what he wants, after all ? Suppose it's too late.

SHELDON. That's a thought you've lived with many years now. You can wait a little longer to find out. (*He moves to* R. *of her.*) Come, lassie, away with you to bed.

HELEN (*moving to the door up* C.). All right. I'll go.

(*She exits up* C., *closing the door behind her.* SHELDON *turns to the fireplace. As he does so, tapping is heard at the french windows. He turns, crosses to the french windows and opens them.* CHARLES *and* HARRISON *enter.*)

CHARLES (*abruptly*). Oh, Sheldon. What a bit of luck ! (*He crosses to* C.) I saw the light across the lawn. Stupid thing—I forgot my key.

(SHELDON *closes the french windows.* HARRISON *moves to the standard lamp and switches it on.*)

What are you doing here at this time of night ?

SHELDON (*easing* L.C.). I thought I heard somebody, Mr Charles. I'm glad you came back.

CHARLES (*moving to* SHELDON). Why shouldn't I come back ?

SHELDON. Is there anything I can get for you ?

CHARLES. I'll have a drink, that's all. You'll have one, I'm sure, John.

HARRISON (*moving to the drinks table*). Thanks, I will. (*He pours out two whiskies.*)

CHARLES. Good—someone's lit the fire. (*To* SHELDON. *Sharply.*) All right, Sheldon—go to bed.

SHELDON (*moving to the door up* C. ; *hurt*). I'm just going, Mr Charles. Good night to you.

(*He glances at both of them, then exits up* C., *closing the door behind him.*)

CHARLES (*moving and sitting on the settee*). Phew ! What a night ! (*He leans back, tired.*) Thank God it's stopped raining.

(HARRISON *moves with the two drinks to* R. *of the settee.*)

HARRISON (*holding out a drink to* CHARLES). Your drink.

(CHARLES *takes a glass.*)

Would you rather I went to bed—or do you want to talk ?

CHARLES. I wish I could. Talking might clear my mind.

HARRISON (*moving and sitting in the chair below the fireplace*). You're all right.

CHARLES. I feel as though I'm suspended between two worlds. This one I've built up all around me—and the one I'm beginning to remember again.

HARRISON. Is it coming back ?

CHARLES. Bits are. I remember leaving Melbury—that was the last hospital. That hospital ! The horror of it. It's so clear that I—I feel I'm going to stammer again and I almost break out in a sweat. I stammered quite a lot—in fact I could hardly talk at all for weeks on end. It was Armistice Day. Did I say that before ?

(HARRISON *nods. There is a pause.*)

There was a fog. I just walked out of the gates—I suppose, in the excitement, the guards had relaxed their watch. I wandered through the crowds, terrified. Terrified of having to speak to anyone and terrified of being recognized and taken back to the hospital. It was too much like an asylum. Full of psychiatrists giving treatments and asking questions. Nothing but questions. You see, I had no idea even of what my name was. I could remember nothing. The authorities knew nothing, either. I was a number from a prison camp. No relatives turned up to claim me. I must have been a pretty bad case. Certainly not fit enough to grapple with the Armistice crowds. I went into a tobacconist's shop—more to get away from the noise than anything. (*He pauses. Simply.*) And she was there.

HARRISON. She ?

CHARLES (*softly*). Yes, the one I've been looking for.

HARRISON. So there was someone ?

CHARLES. Yes. She is the promise—the memory I've almost caught so many times over these years. She took me from the shop, poor stammering bundle of nerves that I was. " You'll never get well in a place like that ", she said. Of course, she guessed that I came from the hospital.

HARRISON. Who was she ?

CHARLES. I don't know. I can't *see* her, but I can remember her warmth—her big-heartedness, the way she gave without stint. I had fever that night and she got me a room in an old pub run by a friend of hers—called Biffer—that's it, Biffer Briggs. The whole place was Bedlam with the celebrations. She wrapped herself round me to keep me warm. " Tell you what, ducky, I'm just like a mother tonight, so cuddle up close." I remember her saying that. And with the warmth and peace of her, I slept all night. (*He rises, puts his glass on the coffee table, and moves* c.) God ! The warmth and peace after those years of horror.

HARRISON. And what happened then ?

CHARLES (*thinking hard*). She must have been on the stage, touring in *Salute The Flag*, that show tonight on the radio. Yes, when I was better she took me along with her and got me a job with the company. I think I was kind of business manager. She used to shield me from everything. Her patience and faith in me cured my stammering, so that I could face the outside world again.

HARRISON. What sort of an acrtess was she ? (*He finishes his drink and places his glass on the coffee table.*)

CHARLES. Ordinary musical stuff and she used to do impersonations. She was good. But that scene in the show tonight—it would be a hellish moment like that, that would bring it all back to me. The actor playing the subaltern was ill and I had to go on for him. Just one line. When I got on to the stage my old stammer came back. It was agony getting that awful line out. I wanted the ground to open. And then groping my way off the stage, with the audience roaring with laughter, the door knob came off in my hand. *That* just finished the audience, they yelled themselves hoarse. (*He pauses, moves up* c., *turns and gets a grip on himself. Casually.*) It was evidently so funny that they kept the gag in all these years.

HARRISON. What did you do ?

CHARLES (*moving* c.). I packed up and walked out. I was numb with humiliation. I didn't realize then to what lengths actors will go to get a laugh. I left no word. I just disappeared. (*He moves to the duet stool and sits.*) But she found me. That was one of the things I always liked about her—the way she always took the initiative. Her name ? (*He buries his face in his hands.*) What was her name ?

HARRISON (*rising and moving to* CHARLES). Relax, sir. Don't worry yourself any more now. Just hang on to the fact there isn't a gap any longer and be satisfied.

CHARLES (*looking up*). Satisfied ? When you say that I wonder if—if you quite realize—what it all amounts to.

HARRISON. Oh, yes, I do. It means you're now completely cured.

CHARLES. You don't really think that's all it amounts to ? You must know there's only one thing that matters—only one thing.

HARRISON. And that is ?

CHARLES (*rising*). I must find her. (*He crosses below the settee.*)

HARRISON. After all these years—it isn't possible.

CHARLES. I must try.

HARRISON (*moving above the settee*). It was up to her, surely, to look for you—yet apparently she never did.

CHARLES. Maybe—maybe not. I don't care. I must find her.

HARRISON. And if by chance—not that I think there is much chance—but just for the sake of argument—if you should find her—what then ?

CHARLES (*simply*). Then I should be happy again.

HARRISON. I know, but there might be—complications.

CHARLES (*moving* L.C.). *Complications ?* You'll be telling me next I ought to consult Truslove.

HARRISON. I'm thinking of Helen. After all, she is your wife. You ought at least to consider her.

CHARLES. Anything I ought to do now is nothing compared with what I ought to have done before.

HARRISON. But that's in the past—irrevocable.

CHARLES. But if she and I can find each other again.

HARRISON. We seem to be talking about different persons. (*He moves to the fire and stands gazing into it.*)

CHARLES (*sitting on the duet stool*). Her name ! If only I could remember her name. I wish I could remember more about her than her warmth, the love, the goodness of her.

(HELEN *enters silently up* C., *and stand just by the door watching, unseen by* CHARLES *and* HARRISON.)

Why can't I remember her name, what she looked like ? It mustn't slip away again, before I've remembered the only thing that matters. (*Frenziedly.*) I'll go mad if I don't remember her. What was her name ? I must think, think. O God, help me to think. It was a name I didn't like at first but got to love. A soft-sounding name—O God, what was it ?

HELEN (*from the shadows by the door* C. ; *whispering softly*). Paula.

HARRISON (*turning*). Paula ! (*He gazes enquiringly at* HELEN.)

CHARLES. Paula ! That was her name. Paula !

(HELEN *motions* HARRISON *to go out. He moves slowly and quietly to the door up* C. *and exits.*)

She was so young and gay. They all adored her. She tracked me down to a cottage at the foot of a mountain. That was the mountain I recognized. It was a picturesque little place with an odd-sounding name. The name ? Oh, I must remember.

HELEN (*softly*). Beachings Over.

CHARLES (*rising and crossing to* R.C.). Beachings Over. That's it. She found I was there and came up after me to the top of the mountain—Mickle ! The joy, the relief, when I realized she *had* found me. I knew then that I loved her. I asked her to marry me when I was better. But we were married right away. That's what she

wanted. And went to live in London. My life began with her.
That's the sense of loss I've had all these years. Then I went on a
night train to Liverpool to see an editor. She saw me off. She was
wearing a bunch of violets. Oh, God, what happened to her?
Perhaps she went back to Beachings Over. That's where she found
me before. Beachings Over and Mickle—with that wonderful view
and much too much sky. A view of four counties.

HELEN. Five, Smithy.

CHARLES. Yes, of course, five. (*He is conscious of* HELEN'S *voice
for the first time.*) Smithy. That's what she used to call me. (*He
turns suddenly and sees* HELEN.) That's what she used to call me.

HELEN. Yes, Smithy.

CHARLES. You !

HELEN (*terrified it's going to be a shock*). Yes.

CHARLES. You, all the time. You've found me again, Paula.

HELEN (*moving* L.C.). I'd always do that, Smithy.

CHARLES. You promised you'd be with me when my memory
came back.

HELEN. I promised.

CHARLES. And all these years you've waited. It's a long time.

HELEN. Yes.

CHARLES (*moving in close to her*). Paula ! Paula, darling ! (*He
takes her in his arms.*)

HELEN (*her face showing over his shoulder*). Oh, Smithy—Smithy,
maybe it's not too late.

CURTAIN

FURNITURE AND PROPERTY LIST

PROLOGUE.

Personal.—HELEN : bunch of violets, handbag. *In it :* handkerchief.
Effects.—Railway guard's whistle.
    Train noises. (H.M.V. effects record E583).

ACT I.

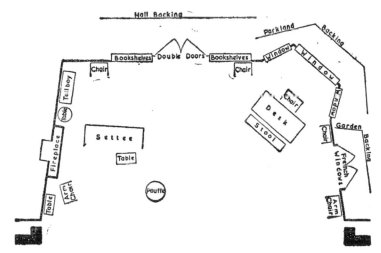

SCENE 1.

On Stage.—Built-in bookshelves. *In them :* books.
    Drinks table. *On it :* tray, decanter of brandy, 4 glasses.
    2 armchairs.
    Settee. *On it :* cushions.
    Pedestal table. *On it :* bowl of flowers.
    Tallboy. *On it :* ornamental vase.
    2 Queen Anne chairs.
    Low coffee table.
    Pouffe.
    Duet stool.
    Desk chair.
    Desk. *On it :* inkstand, blotter, ashtray, cigarette box with
      cigarettes, matches.
    Brass kerb.
    Fire-irons.
    Hearth rug.
    Carpet.
    Curtains.
    Pictures.
    On mantelpiece : gilt and ormulu clock, vases.

76

In hall : table, runner.
3 pairs electric candle wall brackets.
Light switch L. of door.
Bell-push above fireplace.

Set.—*On coffee table :* tea tray, teapot, milk jug, sugar basin, 5 each, cups, saucers, spoons, plates, knives. Large iced cake on plate.

In hearth : kettle stand.

Fire on.
French windows shut.
Wall brackets off.

Off Stage.—Silver kettle of hot water (SHELDON).
Scuttle of coal (ELSIE).
Golf club (GEORGE).

Personal.—JILL : handbag.
TRUSLOVE : snuff-box with snuff, handkerchief.

SCENE 2.

Strike.—Pouffe.
Kettle and stand.
Tea-tray and contents.
From desk : golf club, tea-cup, glass.
Bowl of flowers from pedestal table.
Decanter of brandy, tray and glasses from drinks table.

Set.—Pedestal table L. of settee.
Empty vase on pedestal table.
Glass of whisky on mantelpiece.
Empty decanter on drinks table.

Open curtains.
Open french windows.
Fire off.
Wall brackets off.

Off Stage.—Bunch of roses (LYDIA).
Tray. *On it :* decanter of whisky (ELSIE).
Brief case. *In it :* papers (CHARLES).
Attaché case. *In it :* papers (HELEN).

Personal.—JILL : handbag. *In it :* bundle of cigarette cards.

ACT II.

SCENE 1.

Strike.—Tray, decanters, glasses.
Vase of roses.
Brief case.

Set.—*On desk :* pedestal telephone.
On drinks table : bowl of flowers.
On pedestal table : bowl of flowers.
On coffee table : tray with 2 cups of coffee.
On settee : copy of *The Tatler.*

French windows closed.
Fire on.
Wall brackets off.

Off Stage.—Brief case (CHARLES).
Tray. *On it :* 2 coffee cups and saucers, jug of coffee, sugar basin, milk jug, spoons (SHELDON).
Bunch of violets (KITTY).

Personal.—CHARLES : wallet. *In it :* five-pound note.

SCENE 2.

Strike.—All flowers, all cushions, clock and vases from mantelpiece, everything from desk except telephone and ashtray, all small pictures.
Coffee tray and contents.

Cover with dust sheets.—Settee, desk, armchair down R., armchair down L.
Close french windows.
Close curtains.
Fire off.
Wall brackets off.

Off Stage.—Logs (SHELDON).
Tray. *On it :* 4 cups, 4 saucers, 4 spoons, tea-pot, sugar basin,
milk jug (SHELDON).

Personal.—SHELDON : matches.
HARRISON : cigarette case with cigarettes, matches.

ACT III.

SCENE 1.

Strike.—Armchair from down R.
Armchair from down L.
Pedestal telephone.
Tea tray and contents.

Move.—Pedestal table to above fireplace.
Drinks table from down R. to R. of the door up C.
Chair from R. of door up C. to L. of tallboy.

Set.—Radiogram down R.
Queen Anne chair below fireplace.
Standard lamp above settee.
High-backed wing armchair L. of settee.
Tapestry highback armchair down L.
On desk : hand microphone telephone, inkstand, blotter, table lamp,
copy of *The Tatler.*
In desk drawer : 2 packs playing cards, 4 bridge score pads, 4 pencils.
On drinks table : tray, bottle of Old Napoleon Brandy, 4 brandy
glasses, decanter of whisky, 4 whisky glasses.
On tallboy : vase of flowers.
On pedestal table : bowl of flowers.
On mantelpiece : gilt and ormulu clock, 2 vases.
On coffee table : tray with coffee cups for three.
On settee : 3 cushions.
Replace pictures.
Close curtains of window up L.
Open french windows.
Wall brackets on.
Standard lamp on.
Desk lamp off.
Fire off.

Off Stage.—Syphon of soda (SHELDON).
Billiards cue (DUCHESS).
Card table (SHELDON).
Bunch of chickweed (TRUSLOVE).

Personal.—DUCHESS : cigar, handbag.
HARRISON : wrist watch.

Effects.—Radio dance music (" Sometimes I'm Happy " ⎫ *H.M.V. Record*
(" These Foolish Things " ⎭ *B*8523.

" Salute The Flag."

" Land of Hope and Glory." (H.M.V. Record RAF 1).

" Tipperary." (Columbia Record DB 489).

" Policeman's Holiday." (H.M.V. Record B 8005).

SCENE 2.

Strike.—Card table, cards, score pads, pencils, billiards cue, brandy glasses from coffee table, chickweed from mantelpiece.

Replace 3 chairs.

Wall brackets off.

Standard lamp off.

Desk lamp on.

Close french windows.

Close curtain at french windows.

Fire on.

LIGHTING PLOT

PROLOGUE.

To open.—All lights out.
Cue 1.—At rise of Curtain—raise lights to ¼.
Cue 2.—HELEN : " Come back soon "—dim to blackout.

ACT I.

SCENE 1.

To open.—All lights checked to ¾.
             Grey twilight outside windows.
             Fire on.
             Wall brackets out.
Cue 1.—JILL : " Kitty, please "—commence slow dim of all lights to ¼.
Cue 2.—SHELDON switches on lights—wall brackets and all lights full up.

SCENE 2.

To open.—All lights full up.
             Fire out.
             Wall brackets out.
             Sunshine outside windows.
No cues.

ACT II.

SCENE 1.

To open.—All lights checked to ¾.
             Fire on.
             Wall brackets out.
             Daylight outside windows.
No cues.

SCENE 2.

To open.—All lights out.
             Fire off.
             Wall brackets out.
             Daylight outside windows.
Cue 1.—SHELDON opens curtains of french windows—all lights up to ½.
Cue 2.—SHELDON kneels at fireplace—bring fire on gently.
Cue 3.—SHELDON opens curtains of window up 1.—all lights up to ¾.

ACT III.

SCENE 1.

To open.—All lights checked to ¾.
             Wall brackets on.
             Standard lamp on.
             Desk lamp off.
             Fire off.
             Moonlight outside windows.
Cue 1.—HELEN switches on desk lamp—all lights up to full.

SCENE 2.

To open.—All lights checked to ¼.
             Fire on.
             Wall brackets off.
             Standard lamp off.
             Desk lamp on.
Cue 1.—HARRISON switches on the standard lamp—all lights up to ½.